Table of contents

A note from the author

This small essay was written as part of a study process initiated by the British Council of Churches in 1981 with a view to a conference of the British churches to be held in 1984. The year was chosen because it was recognized that — because of the famous book of that title — 1984 would be a year when people would be asking questions about what is happening to our society. As the result of considerable discussion it was agreed that a longer time was needed for the preparation of such a conference, and that a paper should be written to provoke discussion and possibly to suggest agenda for a number of specialist groups in preparation for a national conference. The following pages were written to meet this need. A first draft was sent to about fifty representative people, thirty of whom sent helpful criticisms and comments. The paper was substantially revised in the light of these and published by the British Council of Churches with the request that it might be widely studied and that comments might be sent either to the author or to the BCC in order to further the process of discussion and clarification of issues.

As the paper is now being reissued by the WCC, it will be important for readers to recognize that it was written for a British discussion. I am particularly grateful for the paper by Wesley Ariarajah which sets the questions I have raised in the wider context of the world-wide interfaith dialogue. I believe that this paper is asking questions which are of much wider importance than the domestic British discussion. I hope that — even if indirectly — they may be found to be useful for others also.

Selly Oak, UK   LESSLIE NEWBIGIN
Advent 1983

I. Is there a future?

In 1936 my wife and I went to India as missionaries. We travelled in a boat which took a full month for the journey, but at every stop along the way we were reminded that the British flag was not far away. At Port Said we bought our pith helmets — allegedly to protect us from the rays of the sun which — inexplicably — became suddenly lethal at that point, but in fact (as we came to realize later) to equip us with the necessary emblem of the "sahib". From the moment we set foot in Bombay we were unquestionably part of the ruling race. We lived in European style. Very occasionally we heard whispered conversations about some Englishman who had "gone native" — cast away the white man's burden and relapsed into the dark world outside the circle of civilization.

Before we left India in 1974 we had become accustomed to the sight of young people from affluent homes in England, France or Germany roaming the streets in tattered and unwashed Indian clothes, having turned their backs on Europe in the hope that — even as beggars — they might find in India something to make life worth living.

In the subsequent years of ministry in England I have often been asked: "What is the greatest difficulty you face in moving from India to England?" I have always answered: "The disappearance of hope." I believe that everyone who has made the same move will bear me out. Even in the most squalid slums of Madras there was always the belief that things could be improved. One could start a night school, or agitate for a water supply, or establish a "Young Men's Progressive Society". In spite of all the disappointments since independence came in 1947, there was still the belief in a better future ahead.

In England, by contrast, it is hard to find any such hope. Apart from those whose lives are shaped by the Christian hope founded on the resurrection of Jesus as the pledge of a new creation, there is little sign among the citizens of this country of the sort of confidence in the future which was certainly present in the earlier years of this century. For the elderly and the middle-aged there is, for the most part, only the hope of keeping reasonably comfortable amid the disintegration of so many of the familiar values. For very

2

many of the young there is only the terrible spectre of nuclear war, with nothing beyond.

What has happened to our civilization which, so recently, was confident that it was "The Coming World Civilization"?[1] There had been, of course, earlier voices warning of the end of western civilization. But these were lone voices, and the message hardly reached the average person. We were confident then, even after the appalling events of the first world war and its aftermath, that "the modern scientific world-view" was a true account of how things are, in contrast to the myths of the uncivilized world, that our science and technology held the key to unlimited progress, that free democratic institutions would establish themselves everywhere, and that our mastery over nature would create a world of wellbeing for all. It was still possible to talk about "progress" as though it were — if not a law of nature — at least a possible and proper goal for our endeavours. Histories were written of every aspect of life on the basis of the belief that "evolution" — understood as movement from the lower to the higher — was the clue to understanding the past and the framework for planning the future.

Today, in spite of some survivals of the older view, the scene has changed almost completely. Science and technology are seen more as threats than as ground for hope. The rise of the "green" movements as significant political forces is the most obvious sign of this shift in perspective. Science, even in its most benign form as medical science, is now regarded with a scepticism unthinkable fifty years ago. Nearly all the great killing diseases have been mastered in principle, yet the burden on health services in all the western nations is outstripping resources. And the most rapidly growing illnesses are — significantly — those which can be classified broadly as mental, illnesses which are related to the collapse of meaning. Politicians, when out of office, continue to claim that they have solutions for our problems, but their claims are viewed with growing scepticism. It is a strange experience to re-read now, near the end of the twentieth century, the writings of

---

1. The title of a book by W.E. Hocking published as late as 1956.

the eighteenth century philosophers who had translated the Christian vision of a heavenly city into a future earthly utopia, who called upon their contemporaries to forget about "God" and put their hope in a blessed future in which would be realized that happiness which is everybody's right and which "God" has never been able to provide. We, who are ourselves that "future" which was their surrogate for God, can only read their writings now with a sorrow which it is hard to express, as though we want to call up the ghosts of that great century and say: "Friends, it was a wonderful dream, but is was only a dream."[2]

It is, no doubt, easy in every age to point to its obvious weaknesses. What is in question here, however, is something more precise. It is the dramatic suddenness with which, in the space of one life-time, our civilization has so completely lost confidence in its own validity. Every culture in every age has its critics. Every culture goes through periods when self-criticism is general. But it is also true that cultures are born and die. The question now is whether our present self-criticism is merely the normal self-questioning of a healthy culture, or whether we are at the point where a culture is approaching death. It seems to me, and I know that I am not alone, that the truth of our present situation is nearer to the second of these alternatives than to the first. What I am calling "our culture" — and I will try to define this more precisely later — has been for the past half-century divided into two streams — eastern and western. Both the Marxism which is the official ideology of the eastern part, and the liberal capitalism of the west, have their proximate source in that movement of thought which its representatives called "the Enlightenment". They both held, in their period of confidence, to belief in a "heavenly city" which would be built here on earth — whether by evolutionary progress or by revolutionary conflict. Both are now reduced to the state of "holding operations", trying to preserve what has been achieved against the forces which threaten to erode it. And (as Langdon Gilkey has pointed

---

2. See *The Heavenly City of the Eighteenth Century Philosophers*, Carl Becker, 1932.

out) it is significant that the only people who still cherish confidence in the future are the dissidents in each camp. The only convinced Marxists are the dissidents in the west, and the only convinced liberals are the dissidents in the east. On both sides of the divide the established powers are reduced to a struggle to defend the status quo. The loss of confidence in the future is expressed eloquently in the mindless folly of the petty vandalism of those who can only express their rage by smashing up the symbols of meaningless affluence, and the equally mindless madness of the nuclear arms race between the super-powers. The mushroom clouds which rose into the sky above the blasted ruins of Hiroshima and Nagasaki have, ever since that day in 1945, hung in menace over the consciousness of modern men and women, posing with fearful poignancy the question: "Is there a future for civilization as we know it?"

II. The roots of modern culture

I have been speaking about "our culture" and I must now try to say what I mean by this phrase. A convenient dictionary definition of the word is as follows: "The sum total of ways of living built up by a human community and transmitted from one generation to another." Culture thus includes the whole life of human beings in so far as it is a shared life. It includes the science, art, technology, politics, jurisprudence and religion of a group of people. Fundamental to any culture is language which embodies the way in which a people grasps and copes with experience, sharing it with one another within the group. So long as one lives one's life within one culture, one is hardly aware of the way in which language provides the framework in which experience is placed, the spectacles through which one "sees". It is when one lives in a completely different culture and learns a new language that one discovers that there are other ways of grasping experience and coping with it. One discovers that things are seen differently through different spectacles. When, as happened during the past two centuries, the culture of western Europe invaded the cultures of what we now call the "third world", an essential element in that invasion was the introduction of European languages as media of education. As a result, for example, whole generations in India have grown up with English as their language of public life, and have therefore become accustomed to grasping and coping with experience through the categories of European thought instead of those developed in the ancient cultural traditions of India.

But this European culture which has so forcibly inserted itself into almost every culture of the world is a relatively recent arrival on the stage of history. During most of the history of the world of which we have knowledge, the tribes inhabiting the western peninsulas of Asia have been surpassed in the arts of the civilization by the peoples of India, China and the Arab world. Yet during the past three centuries the descendants of these same tribes have extended their culture into every part of the world, dominating and often destroying more ancient cultures, and creating for the first time a common civilization which embraces the whole earth — not in the sense that it includes everyone, but in the sense that it has a dominating role, at least in nearly all the great cities of the world. To most of the world's people it has appeared as the bearer of "modernity" — with all its implications of technical mastery and unlimited powers of discovery, innovation and control.

W.E. Hocking, writing in 1956, could still speak with unshaken confidence of the almost timeless and universal validity of this culture:

> Today we seem to be standing on the threshold of a new thing, civilization in the singular... For the first time our entire world-space is permeated with ideas which, as Locke said about truth and the keeping of faith, "belong to man as man and not as a member of a society". Here and there in the Orient there is still revulsion from the clinging localisms of western thought and practice, but none towards what we may call the Clean Universals, the sciences, the mathematics, the technics — these it claims not as borrowings from the west, but as its own. In giving birth to the universal, the west has begotten something which can never again be private property.[3]

Hocking's words express the assurance of a culture which was still confident of the universal validity of its way of seeing things. Today we are required to look afresh at this "way of seeing things" which is in fact being questioned, and to enquire about its origins and credentials.

I have referred to the eighteenth century "Enlightenment" as the proximate source of our culture, but of course its roots lie much further back in history. All movements of thought are continuous because the thinkers live through the changes, even when the changes are as sharp as wars and revolutions. Any decision about where to mark the emergence of something new must be somewhat arbitrary. The movement of which we are speaking had its earlier beginnings in the ferment of thought introduced into western Europe by the translation of Arabic writings into Latin, the impact of Aristotelian

---

3. *Op. cit.*, pp. 51f.

philosophy, the flood of classical ideas at the time of the Renaissance, the passionate debates of the Reformation, and the beginnings of modern science in the seventeenth century. But it is clear that by the middle of the eighteenth century there was a widespread feeling that Europe had reached a turning point. Developments which had been going on continuously for several centuries seemed to have reached a point of clarification such that people could only use the word "enlightenment" to describe what had happened. Light had dawned. Darkness had passed away. What had been obscure was now clear. Things would henceforth be seen as they really are. "Enlightenment" is a word with profound religious overtones. It is the word used to describe the decisive experience of the Buddha. It is the word used in the Johannine writings to describe the coming of Jesus: "The light has come into the world" (John 3:19). The leading thinkers of the mid-eighteenth century felt themselves to be at such a moment of enlightenment, and this moment provides a proper point from which to begin an understanding of our culture.

The feeling of the time is well expressed in some words of D'Alembert, written in 1759:

> If one examines carefully the mid-point of the century in which we live, the events which excite us or at any rate occupy our minds, our customs, our achievements, and even our diversions, it is difficult not to see that in some respects a very remarkable change in our ideas is taking place, a change whose rapidity seems to promise an even greater transformation to come. Natural science from day to day accumulates new riches. Geometry, by extending its limits, has borne its torch into the regions of physical science which lay nearest at hand. The true system of the world has been recognized, developed, and perfected... In short, from the earth to Saturn, from the history of the heavens to that of insects, natural philosophy has been revolutionized; and nearly all other fields of knowledge have assumed new forms... The discovery and application of a new method of philosophizing, the kind of enthusiasm which accompanies discoveries, a certain exaltation of ideas which the spectacle of the universe produces in us — all these causes have brought about a lively fermentation of minds. Spreading

through nature in all directions like a river which has burst its dams, this fermentation has swept with a sort of violence everything along with it which stood in its way.[4]

By the end of the century the leading thinkers in western Europe were convinced that a light had indeed dawned compared with which the preceding centuries of European history and the previous history of most of the human race were darkness. Whatever might have been the achievements of the Greeks and the Chinese, they had not progressed. Modern Europe had surpassed them all. The European peoples were now the vanguard of history. They had mastered the secret of a true scientific method which would banish old superstition and lay bare the real nature of things as in the light of day. They were the bearers of light in a world still largely dark. They had therefore both the duty and the capacity to carry their civilization into every corner of the world. And they proceeded to do so.

What, exactly, was it that happened at that momentous turning point? The French historian Paul Hazard[5] describes it as the replacement of a society based on duties by a society based on rights. That, as we shall note later, is part of the truth, but it is not the root of the matter. Basil Willey has, it seems to me, come much closer to the real answer when he says that the feeling of exhilaration which so manifestly marked the birth of modern European culture came from the conviction that things which had previously been obscure were now being "explained". In place of "dogmatic" or "unscientific" explanations which no longer satisfied the mind, the "true explanation" of things was now coming to light. That was the heart of the matter, says Willey, and that was why "enlightenment" was felt to be such an appropriate word at the point when this movement became fully conscious of itself.

But we have to go on to ask: What do we mean by "explanation"? Basil Willey tries to answer this question:

---

4. D'Alembert, *Eléments de philosophie* (1759), quoted in Ernst Cassirer, *The Philosophy of the Enlightenment*, ET Princeton University Press, 1951.
5. *European Thought*, 1680-1720.

The clarity of an explanation seems to depend upon the degree of satisfaction that it affords. An explanation "explains" best when it meets some need of our nature, some deep-seated demand for assurance. "Explanation" may perhaps be roughly defined as a restatement of something — event, theory, doctrine, etc. — in terms of the current interests and assumptions. It satisfies, as explanation, because it appeals to that particular set of assumptions, as superseding those of a past age or of a former state of mind. Thus it is necessary, if an explanation is to seem satisfactory, that its terms should seem ultimate, incapable of further analysis. Directly we allow ourselves to ask "What, after all, does this explanation amount to?" we have really demanded an explanation of the explanation, that is to say, we have seen that the terms of the first explanation are not ultimate, but can be analyzed into other terms — which perhaps for the moment do seem to us to be ultimate. Thus, for example, we may choose to accept a psychological explanation of a metaphysical proposition, or we may prefer a metaphysical explanation of a psychological proposition. All depends upon our presuppositions, which in turn depend upon our training, whereby we have come to regard (or to feel) one set of terms as ultimate, the other not. An explanation commands our assent with immediate authority when it presupposes the "reality", the "truth", of what seems to us most real, most true. One cannot, therefore, define "explanation" absolutely; one can only say that it is a statement which satisfies the demands of a particular time or place.[6]

If one has lived at different times in different places, one becomes aware of the relativity of all "explanations". One of the first things I did on arrival in India was to be involved in a bus accident which laid me off for two years. How to "explain" it? The Indian pastor said: "It is the will of God." A Hindu would have said: "The karma of your former lives has caught up with you." In some cultures the explanation would be that an enemy had put a curse on me. If I, as an "enlightened" European, had said that it was because the brakes were not working properly, that would have been — for the others — no explanation at all. It would have been simply a re-statement of what had to be explained. To speak of an "explanation" is to speak of the

---

6. *The Seventeenth Century Background*, 1934, pp. 10f.

ultimate framework of axioms and assumptions by means of which one "makes sense of things". "Explanations" only operate within an accepted framework which does not itself require explanation. What happened at the Enlightenment was that one framework was felt to be inadequate and another took its place.

It is because the "Enlightenment" framework is now proving inadequate that we are enabled to look critically at it, and that we are obliged to do so.

What was the "framework" which enabled the thinkers of the eighteenth century to feel satisfied with a new "explanation" of experience? I realize that it is foolish to oversimplify profound and complex movements of thought, but surely it is safe to begin the answer by referring to the enormous impression created on the eighteenth century mind by the work of scientists, and very specially by that of Isaac Newton. Alexander Pope's famous lines express what the eighteenth century felt:

> Nature and Nature's laws lay hid in night.
> God said: "Let Newton be", and all was light.

Newton did not begin from alleged revelation or alleged "innate ideas". He began from observation of the phenomena, and sought thus to formulate general "laws", subsuming the largest possible range of phenomena. The outcome of this method was a picture of the world which was to dominate European thinking for the next two hundred years. In this picture, the "real" world is a world of moving bodies which have a totally "objective" existence apart from any human observer. All reality is ultimately intelligible in these terms. The most fundamental of all "laws" are those of mathematics which are applicable to all that really is. By analyzing all the data of experience into the smallest possible components one can discover the laws which govern their movements and mutual relations. Analysis is the necessary instrument of all thinking and enables human thought to penetrate behind appearances and so discover how things really are. This enterprise is cumulative and infinite in its range. It leads on to a steadily growing capacity to exploit the processes of nature for human ends.

The totality of all observable phenomena is "Nature". "Nature" in effect replaces the concept of God, which is no longer necessary. The characteristic position of the eighteenth century, known as "Deism", did indeed retain the concept of God as a sort of Prime Mover standing behind the processes of nature. But even in that century there were plenty of critics who defined a deist as "a person who is not weak enough to be a Christian and not strong enough to be an atheist". The nineteenth century drew the obvious conclusion: there was no place for "God".

Since "Nature" has replaced "God", the scientist who is learned in the ways of nature becomes the priest who can mediate between the human person and this new god. It is science alone which can enable men and women to understand nature, and can unlock nature's bounty for the benefit of humanity. And science cannot accept any authority other than the authority of the observable facts. Therefore the different sciences, while sharing a common method, are all autonomous as regards their own subject matter. No alleged revelation can be allowed to interfere. The study of astronomy or of biology or of literature (including that segment of literature which has been canonized as "The Word of God") is to be pursued according to the scientific principles of which Newton's physics provide the most brilliant example. Economics (and here the Enlightenment was to have perhaps its most far-reaching consequences) is no longer a part of ethics and therefore ultimately dependent on theology; it is an autonomous science for which ethical principles derived from alleged divine revelation can have no authority.[7, 8]

---

7. The very important shift in this respect from the seventeenth to the eighteenth century is described by Cassirer as follows: "The systematic concepts developed by seventeenth century metaphysics are still firmly anchored in theological thinking with all their originality and independence. For Descartes and Malebranche and for Spinoza and Leibniz there is no solution of the problem of truth independently of the problem of God because knowledge of the divine being forms the highest principle of knowledge from which all other certainties are deduced. But in eighteenth century thought the intellectual centre of gravity changes its position. The various fields of knowledge — natural science, history, law, politics, art — gradually withdraw from the

The replacement of "God" by "Nature" involved a new understanding of "Law". There is no longer a divine law-giver whose commands are to be obeyed because they are God's. Laws are the necessary relationships which spring from the nature of things (Montesquieu). As such they are available for discovery by human reason. Reason is a faculty common to all human beings and is in principle the same everywhere. Provided it is not perverted by the imposition of dogmas from without, reason is capable of discovering what the nature of things is and what — therefore — are "Nature's laws". The most dangerous and destructive of all the dogmas which have perverted human reason is the dogma of original sin. To destroy this wicked slander against humanity is the first essential for the liberating of human reason and conscience to do their proper work. But this dogma is only the centre-piece of a whole structure of dogma which has to be destroyed. Any authority — of dogma, of scripture or of "God" — which purports to replace human reason is to be rejected as false and as a treason against the dignity of the human being.

The word "dignity" is used advisedly. The mediaeval world spoke of a person's "honour", and this was related to his or her status in society.[9] After the Enlightenment one spoke of human "dignity" — something which belongs to every human being simply from the person's birth and apart

---

domination and tutelage of traditional metaphysics and theology. They no longer look to the concept of God for their justification and legitimation; the various sciences themselves now determine that concept on the basis of their specific form. The relations between the concept of God and the concepts of truth, morality, law are by no means abandoned, but their direction changes. An exchange of index symbols takes place, as it were. That which formerly had established other concepts, now moves into the position of that which is to be established, and that which hitherto had justified other concepts, now finds itself in the position of a concept which requires justification. Finally even the theology of the eighteenth century is affected by this trend. It gives up the absolute primacy it had previously enjoyed; it no longer sets the standard but submits to certain basic norms derived from another source which are furnished it by reason as the epitome of independent intellectual forces." *Op. cit.*, pp. 158f.

8. Cassirer, *op. cit.*, p. 163.
9. See *The Homeless Mind*, Peter Berger *et al.*, 1973, Chapter 3 Excursus.

from any question of social status. Every human being is possessed of reason and conscience, and is therefore capable of distinguishing truth from error, right from wrong. In this sense, every human being is "autonomous", not subject to an external law-giver, ruling his or her own life in accordance with the real "laws" — which are the laws of nature discoverable by the exercise of reason and the moral law which is written in the conscience of every person. In the later developments which followed the Enlightenment (and reacted against some of its features) this vision of the autonomous human person became more and more important. The Romantic Movement developed the idea of the "personality", and it became part of the unquestioned assumptions of a western European that every human person has the "right" to develop his or her own potential to the greatest possible extent, limited only by the parallel rights of others. Mediaeval society had emphasized the idea of the duties involved for each person by his or her position in society. From the Enlightenment onwards, it was the "rights of man" which seemed axiomatic. To the founding fathers of the new republic created in the New World to embody the principles of this new philosophy, it seemed necessary and natural to begin with the famous words: "We hold these truths to be self-evident, that all men are created equal, that they are endowed by their Creator with certain inalienable rights; that among these are life, liberty and the pursuit of happiness; that to secure these rights governments are instituted among men, deriving their just powers from the consent of the governed." The rights of the human person are the unquestioned starting point from which all else follows.

These rights include the right to the pursuit of "happiness". Happiness (bonheur) was hailed by the eighteenth century philosophers as "a new word in Europe". In place of the joys of heaven to which the mediaeval person was encouraged to look forward, Enlightenment people looked forward to "happiness" here on earth. This would come within the reach of all through the cumulative work of science, liberating societies from bondage to dogma and superstition, unlocking the secrets of nature and opening

them for all. Once again Pope is the spokesman of his
age:

> Oh happiness, Our Being's End and Aim.
> Good, Pleasure, Ease, Content, Whate'er thy Name.

Hannah Arendt[10] has pointed out that, for some at least
of the American founding fathers, the happiness intended
was the "public happiness" of actively shared responsibility
for public life. She also shows, however, that while any sort
of private hedonism was very far from their purposes, the
course of events led inexorably to an interpretation of their
language as meaning the pursuit of private wellbeing. The
result is that the world becomes (as in the contemporary
western world it has become) a place where each individual
has the "right" to pursue "happiness" in the domestic and
privatized sense, and it is the responsibility of the state to
see that this right is honoured. It follows, of course, that
any consideration of what lies beyond death is both
unreliable and subversive. It is unreliable because the
methods of science do not provide any reliable knowledge
of what lies beyond death. It is subversive because it deflects
attention from the "happiness" which is the right of every
person in this life, to an alleged happiness in another life for
which we have only the authority of the clergy who
themselves live very comfortably in this life at the expense
of the unenlightened poor.

Once the concept of "human rights" has established itself
as an axiom, the question inevitably arises: How and by
whom are these rights to be secured? With growing emphasis, post-Enlightenment societies have answered: by the
state. The nation state, replacing the old concepts of the
Holy Church and the Holy Empire, is the centre-piece in the
political scene in post-Enlightenment Europe. After the
trauma of the religious wars of the seventeenth century,
Europe settled down to the principle of religious co-
existence, and the passions which had formerly been invested in rival interpretations of religion were more and
more invested in the nation state. Nationalism became the

---

10. *On Revolution*, 1963, Chapter 3.

effective ideology of the European peoples, always at times of crises proving stronger than any other ideological or religious force. If there is any entity to which ultimate loyalty is due, it is the nation state. In the twentieth century we have become accustomed to the fact that — in the name of the nation — Catholics will fight Catholics, Protestants will fight Protestants, and Marxists will fight Marxists. The charge of blasphemy, if it is ever made, is treated as a quaint anachronism; but the charge of treason, of placing another loyalty above that to the nation state, is treated as the unforgivable crime. The nation state has taken the place of God. Responsibilities for education, healing and public welfare which had formerly rested with the Church devolved more and more upon the nation state. In the present century this movement has been vastly accelerated by the advent of the "welfare state". National governments are widely assumed to be responsible for and capable of providing those things which former generations thought only God could provide — freedom from fear, hunger, disease and want — in a word: "happiness".

If it is true that we are now compelled to look critically at the "conversion" which brought our modern world into existence, it would be perverse and misleading to do so without first acknowledging our enormous debt to the Enlightenment. One cannot fail, even now, to be moved by the words in which Immanuel Kant answered the question: "What is Enlightenment?" "Enlightenment is man's exodus from his self-incurred tutelage. Tutelage is the inability to use one's understanding without the guidance of another person... 'Dare to know' (*sapere aude*)! Have the courage to use your own understanding; this is the motto of the Enlightenment." * Who can deny the liberating consequences which flowed from this robust summons? For Christians it is particularly necessary to acknowledge that the Bible and the teaching office of the Church had become fetters upon the human spirit; that the removal of barriers to freedom of conscience and of intellectual enquiry was achieved by the leaders of the Enlightenment against the

---

* See note 8, p. 12.

resistance of the churches; that this made possible the ending of much cruelty, oppression and ignorance; and that the developments in science and technology which this liberation has made possible have brought vast benefit to succeeding generations. It would be dishonest to fail to recognize our debt to the Enlightenment.

Moreover there is much to be said for the view that the unfinished work of the Enlightenment is still a large part of our contemporary agenda. The leaders of the Enlightenment by no means completed the tasks they set themselves. They were not exempt from the human sin which invokes eternal truths to justify selfish interests. The "human rights" which the eighteenth century philosophers espoused were mainly the rights of the rising bourgeoisie. Freedom meant primarily freedom to hold property, to trade and to travel. It was not freedom for workers to organize trade unions, for blacks to vote, for Aboriginal peoples to retain their lands, or for women to have equal rights with men. Late in the twentieth century we are still struggling with this unfinished agenda.

Yet epochs in history always overlap, and while we work to complete the unfinished business of the Enlightenment, we have also — I believe — to recognize that its way of understanding the world can no longer satisfy us. The "explanations" of the eighteenth century no longer provide meaning for us. We have, beyond this unfinished agenda, the new task of seeking an understanding of "how things are" which will meet our sense of being at a dead end and open new horizons of meaning.

III. A new framework

In the preceding section I have tried, in very crude outline, to sketch the framework of "self-evident" truths which, since the Enlightenment, has governed the way in which modern western peoples have grasped and coped with experience. Inevitably — writing in the year 1983 — I have implied that for us in this day these things are no longer self-evident. The expectations of the eighteenth century have not been realized. The heavenly city has not arrived, and we no longer expect it. Science has won victories beyond the dreams of the eighteenth century, but the world which results does not appear to us to be a more rational world than that of previous centuries. More and more people among the most powerful nations on earth feel themselves helpless in the grip of irrational forces. Irrespective of the divide between "east" and "west", there is profound scepticism about what governments can achieve. The modern techniques of communication and control give governments more and more apparent power, but this is met by more and more sophisticated forms of resistance by groups which demand their rights. There is consequently a spiralling escalation of violence — terrorism on one side and the use of torture on the other. Obscene cruelties which the eighteenth century philosophers relegated to the dark ages are now practised by "civilized" governments. And among those who are not directly involved in terrorism or in torture, there is a profound sense of meaninglessness, of "anomie", leading from the pathetic question of young people in the rich world: "Who am I", to the mindless vandalism in the streets of our affluent cities. The Paris students, in the heady days of the 1968 revolution, had among their graffiti the slogan: "We reject the alternatives — to die of starvation or to die of boredom." Thousands of their successors roam through India in search of "meaning" — and find both of these things from which they flee.[11]

The liberation of our rational faculties from the control of "dogma" has not, apparently, led us into a world which is rational, which is (to use a word whose popularity is significant) "meaningful". We are once again at a point where

---

11. See *Karma-Cola*, Gita Meta, 1980.

accepted "explanations" no longer explain. When my Indian bus crashed into an iron gate and broke the passengers' legs, my "explanation" that the brakes had failed was no explanation to the Indian pastor. And he was right. Science has traced the "laws of nature" ("the necessary relations between things") with a daring and a rigour that are among the greatest achievements of the human spirit. But the result is a world without meaning. Why, otherwise, is astrology such a burgeoning industry in the most "advanced" countries of the west? The "explanations" which science provides no longer explain. One might trace the failure of the brakes through an endless regress of causes back to the creation of the world itself, but that would not explain why I happened to be the one whose leg was broken just at the start of a missionary career. How can this event be meaningful for me? That is a question which "science" does not ask and does not pretend to answer.

At this point we have to face, I believe, the fact that our problems will not be solved within the terms provided by our culture. As heirs of the Enlightenment and representatives of the "modern scientific world-view", our normal procedure is to list a series of "problems", identify their causes, and then propose "solutions" based on a scientific analysis of the situation. We normally proceed on the assumption that there must in principle be a solution which proper research can identify and proper techniques can deliver. Today we are becoming sceptical about this approach. We are coming to see that there are "problems" in human life for which there are no "solutions". The question has to be asked whether we do not need new models for understanding our human situation. This means that we have to re-examine our accepted framework of understanding. The pre-condition for effective action in any field is a true perception of how things are. Our culture has been confident, during the past two centuries, that it could change the world. Perhaps we may now have to insist that the point is to understand it.

In our brief look at the movement of thought which saw itself as the dawning of light in darkness, we saw how often the word "dogma" appeared among the obstacles to the free exercise of reason. In the older Christian tradition "dogma" was a good word. It stood for the blessed gift of an assured truth on which we could rely. "Doubt", on the other hand, stood for something evil, something of which the symbol was the sin of Adam and Eve in doubting the goodness of God's prohibition against eating the fruit of the tree of knowledge of good and evil. According to the biblical story, the primal sin, which was the root of all that followed, was the willingness to entertain a suspicion that God could not be wholly trusted, and therefore to wish to see for oneself what God had hidden. The limit which God had set was — according to the Genesis saga — an invitation to trust. Evil is what God has not willed; his will is that men and women should know only good. But if God is not to be trusted, then men and women must be able to look at both sides and make up their own minds. Thus, says the tempter, "your eyes will be opened and you will be like God, knowing good and evil" (Gen. 3:5). In this way of understanding the human situation, faith — in the sense of loving trust — is the primary virtue and doubt is the primal sin.

The Enlightenment reversed the roles of the two words "Doubt" was elevated to a position of honour as the first principle of knowledge. The readiness to question all accepted opinions was the prime condition for arriving at the truth. "Dogma", on the other hand, became a bad word, standing for all that shackles the free exercise of human reason. And so it has remained to this day. Few contemporary English theologians like to hear their discipline referred to by its traditional name —"Dogmatics". The reversal of roles between these two words was at the heart of the experience which ushered in the modern scientific world-view. To look at what was implied in this reversal will help us to understand the situation in which we now stand.

The people of the Enlightenment saw doubt as a necessary weapon in the battle against "superstition". The great enemy of knowledge was the superstitious belief which refused to submit itself to rational doubt. There was a work of demolition to be done, bringing the weapons of observation, analysis and critical reason to bear on dogmas which had been accepted on the authority of the ancients, or the *epistemology*

alleged authority of revelation. And, once again, we have to acknowledge our debt to the Enlightenment for breaking the power of many ancient superstitions. Yet doubt can only be secondary, not primary in the activity of knowing. The critical faculty can only operate on the basis of beliefs which are — in the moment of critical questioning — unquestioned. It is impossible to doubt all one's beliefs at the same time without falling into imbecility.

All understanding of how things are has to begin with an act of attention in which we deliberately open ourselves to attend to something particular in the total environment of which we are always vaguely aware. This primal act is an act of faith. We have no means of knowing in advance that the thing is worth attending to. Whether it is a sight, a sound, a sensation, a verbal report, or whatever, we have to begin by an act of attending to what is there. This is an action of "receiving". But in order to "receive" we have to relate it in some way to the experience we already have. Only in this way does it have meaning. But in this act of relating, we are obliged to ask questions. This thing newly apprehended may call into question, or be called into question by, the experience we already have. Without this element of questioning, in fact of doubting, there can be no secure knowledge of how things are. We are at the mercy of superstition. Yet the critical faculty which enables us to question any belief is itself dependent upon beliefs which provide the grounds for our questioning. Doubt, therefore, is essential but secondary in the enterprise of knowing how things are. What is primary is the act of attending and receiving, and this is an action of faith.

At the centre of the movement which created our modern culture was a shift in the balance between faith and doubt. After a very long period in which the European perception of how things are was controlled by a dogma based on divine revelation, the principle of doubt reasserted itself in the famous phrase "Dare to know". And who can deny that the result has been fruitful beyond the dreams of those who first used this slogan? Why, then, do we now find ourselves at what feels like a dead-end? Why has life become meaningless for so many in our culture? In a vivid parable Michael Polanyi has suggested the answer:

Polanyi etc.

The critical movement which seems to be nearing the end of its course today was perhaps the most fruitful effort ever sustained by the human mind. The past four or five centuries, which have gradually destroyed or overshadowed the whole mediaeval cosmos, have enriched us mentally and morally to an extent unrivalled by any period of similar duration. But its incandescence has fed on the combustion of the Christian heritage in the oxygen of Greek rationalism, and when the fuel was exhausted, the critical framework itself burnt away.[12]

Polanyi goes on to quote Locke's definition of faith as "a persuasion of our minds short of knowledge", and continues:

Here lies the break by which the critical mind repudiated one of its two cognitive faculties and tried completely to rely on the remainder. Belief was so thoroughly discredited that, apart from specially privileged opportunities, such as may still be granted to the holding and profession of religious beliefs, modern man lost his capacity to accept any explicit statement as his own belief. All belief was reduced to the status of subjectivity: to that of an imperfection by which knowledge fell short of universality.[13]

I intend to follow Polanyi in the next stage of his argument when he calls for a "post-critical philosophy" as the necessary starting point for the renewal of our culture, but before doing so I want to pick up the important point which Polanyi makes when he speaks of the "specially privileged opportunities" which were granted to religious belief in the "modern" world. The point he makes here is vital for the understanding of our situation.

The mediaeval world-view, based on the Christian dogma, was one which embraced the whole life of society, public as well as private. It had as much to do with economics and social order as with prayer and the sacraments. Like the Bible, it assumed that human life is to be understood in its totality, that is to say as a life in which there is no dichotomy between the private and the public, between the believer and the citizen.

---

12. *Personal Knowledge*, 1958, pp. 265f.
13. *Ibid.*, p. 266.

amazing! it had actually been fractured by the Reformation!!!

The story of the Church's attempt to respond to the challenge of the Enlightenment is — of course — complex. Western Christendom had already been fragmented by the failure of the Reformation to capture the whole Church. From the beginning there were voices which challenged the new direction of thought. Perhaps the only one of these which is now remembered is that of Pascal. At the inevitable risk of over-simplification one may say that while the Roman Catholic Church put up defensive barriers against the Enlightenment, the Protestant churches gradually surrendered the public sphere to control by the assumptions of the Enlightenment and survived by retreating into the private sector. The typical form of living Christian faith in its Protestant forms from the eighteenth century onwards was pietism, a religion of the soul, of the inner life, of personal morals and of the home. The Church did indeed struggle to keep the sphere of education within the old framework, but it was not successful. First the universities and then the schools became purely "secular" in their presuppositions. The condition for university entrance was no longer acceptance of the Christian dogmatic framework; it was acceptance of the framework provided by the ideas of the Enlightenment. Christian faith became — for most people — a private and domestic matter strictly separated from the public worlds of politics and economics. The Bible no longer provided the framework within which world history was understood. World history was now taught as the history of civilization with — quite naturally — the civilization of western Europe as its climax. The other way of understanding history, which found its climax in the person of a first century Jew, was relegated to a separate department of "religious instruction" and treated as a parable of the history of the human soul.

The peaceful co-existence of Christianity with the post-Enlightenment culture which this secured has endured so long that it is hard for the Church now to recover the standpoint for a genuinely missionary approach to our "modern" culture. When the Gospel is brought for the first time into contact with a culture previously shaped by another vision, the missionary has to be aware of the differences between

This model is in my view incorrect. The picture should not be of Christian culture vs other culture — it never has been like that — but of Christian culture transforming other culture from within.

the two "frameworks" and to find ways of making the message intelligible and challenging to the other culture as a whole. The missionary will seek to avoid two pitfalls. One is so to fail to understand the culture that the message appears irrelevant. The other danger is to accept the culture in such an uncritical way that the message is simply absorbed without posing a radical challenge. The second situation is what is often described as syncretism. It would be hard to deny that contemporary British (and most of western) Christianity is an advanced case of syncretism. The Church has lived so long as a permitted and even privileged minority, accepting relegation to the private sphere in a culture whose public life is controlled by a totally different vision of reality, that it has almost lost the power to address a radical challenge to that vision and therefore to "modern western civilization" as a whole. Looking at the world missionary situation as a whole, this failure is the most important and the most serious factor in the whole world situation, because this western culture has penetrated into every other culture in the world and threatens to destabilize them all.

Reference to the privileged position of Christianity as an optional private opinion held under the shadow of another world-view leads us back to the argument of Polanyi. Recognizing and prizing the immense achievements of our modern culture, he claims that the time has come for a shift in the balance between faith and doubt in the whole enterprise of understanding, a recognition that doubt — though always an essential ingredient — is always secondary and that faith is fundamental. His book is a massive attempt to demonstrate that all knowledge of reality rests upon faith-commitments which cannot be demonstrated but are held by communities whose "conviviality" is a necessary factor in the enterprise of knowing. This is as true for the scientist as for the Christian believer. Polanyi therefore pleads for a "post-critical philosophy" as the necessary condition for the renewal of our culture.

As an indication of what is now needed he evokes the memory of Augustine whose work "brought the history of Greek philosophy to a close by inagurating for the first time

24

a post-critical philosophy".[14] This example is particularly relevant to our time because the "turn" which brought Europe into its modern period of brilliance was the opposite of that effected by Augustine; it was a turn away from the Christian dogma to the spirit and method of the pre-Christian classical world. In his book *Christianity and Classical Culture* (1940), Charles Norris Cochrane has told the story of the decay and disintegration of classical culture from the time of its glory under Augustus to the time when it had ceased to provide a meaningful framework for living and was replaced by a new framework which (for western Christendom) was articulated by St Augustine. What Augustine offered was a "post-critical philosophy" in the sense that it began with the revelation of God in Jesus Christ and claimed that the acceptance by faith of this revelation provided the starting point for the endless enterprise of understanding. The revelation furnished a new framework for grasping and coping with experience. It overcame the old dichotomies from which classical thought could not escape — the unbridgeable division through all reality between the "sensible" and the "intelligible" (corresponding to the modern division between "material" and "spiritual"), and the irrationality that turned all human history into a conflict between "virtue" and "fortune" — between human courage and skill on the one hand and the blind power of fate on the other. The revelation of God in Jesus Christ, articulated in the doctrine of the Trinity, provided a way of understanding which overcame these dichotomies. To accept the trinitarian model means to believe that the power which rules all events in the visible world and the power that can illuminate and fortify the inner person is one with the man who went his humble way from Bethlehem to Calvary in the days of Pontius Pilate. The starting point for this new understanding was faith. Augustine quotes Isaiah: "Unless you believe you will not understand" (7:9). Faith is not a terminus but a starting point from which understanding can begin. This model is offered for acceptance by faith as the way to understanding. Its motto is *Credo ut intelligam*, I believe in order that I may understand.

---

14. *Ibid.*, p. 266.

There are obvious parallels between our situation and that of Augustine. We stand at what feels like the end of a period of extraordinary brilliance. The feeling of being "at the end" is — as I have suggested — the feeling that our culture has no future and that life therefore has no meaning. The classical culture which was disintegrating in Augustine's day was the one to which the Enlightenment sought to return. It was the vision of the Greek philosophers and the Roman law-givers, not that of the biblical prophets and apostles, which inspired the age of which we are the heirs. If we too have come to a point where our culture seems to have no future, if our young people are tempted to turn their backs on the whole magnificent European adventure and seek for meaning among the a-historical mysticisms of Asia, if the immense achievements of autonomous reason seem to have produced a world which is at best meaningless and at worst full of demons, then it could be that Polanyi is right, that we shall not find renewal within the framework of the assumptions which the Enlightenment held to be "self-evident", that there is needed a radical conversion, a new starting point which begins as an act of trust in divine grace as something simply given to be received in faith and gratitude.

But, of course, we can never simply repeat history. Augustine can provide an analogy but not a model. If we follow Polanyi in asking for a "post-critical philosophy" as the pre-condition for the renewal of our culture, if we claim that we today must again be ready to stake our whole future on consciously a-critical statements, this can only be in the full acknowledgment of the irreversible nature of our experience in the past 250 years. On this point Polanyi writes:

> This invitation to dogmatism may appear shocking; yet it is but the corollary to the greatly increased critical powers of man. These have endowed our mind with a capacity for self-transcendence of which we can never again divest ourselves. We have plucked from the Tree a second apple which has for ever imperilled our knowledge of Good and Evil, and we must learn to know these qualities henceforth in the blinding light of our new analytical powers. Humanity has been deprived a second time of its innocence, and driven out of another garden which

was, at any rate, a Fool's Paradise. Innocently, we had trusted that we could be relieved of all personal responsibility for our beliefs by objective criteria of validity — and our own critical powers have shattered this hope. Struck by our sudden nakedness, we may try to brazen it out by flaunting it in a profession of nihilism. But modern man's immorality is unstable. Presently his moral passions reassert themselves in objectivist disguise and the scientistic Minotaur is born.

The alternative to this, which I am seeking to establish here, is to restore to us once more the power for the deliberate holding of unproven beliefs. We should be able to profess now knowingly and openly those beliefs which could be tacitly taken for granted in the days before modern philosophic criticism reached its present incisiveness. Such powers may appear dangerous. But a dogmatic orthodoxy can be kept in check both internally and externally, while a creed inverted into a science is both blind and deceptive.[15]

The Christian Church has, of course, always offered to men and women a Gospel which cannot be demonstrated but can be accepted in faith. In what sense, then, is Polanyi asking for anything new? The answer to that question is of crucial importance, and it is as follows. Our culture has acknowledged and protected the right of individuals to hold this faith as a private option. But it has drawn a sharp distinction between this private option and the principles which govern public life. These principles belong to the realm of "public truth", that is to say to the area which is governed by the truths which are either held to be self-evident or can be shown to be true to any person who is willing to consider all the evidence. In the popular use of the word "scientific", they are the things which can be "scientifically" demonstrated and which all reasonable people therefore ought to accept. But they also include those beliefs which cannot be demonstrated but have nevertheless been held for so long to be "self-evident" that they are rarely subjected to critical questioning. Essentially they are those which we have identified in our brief look at the thought of the eighteenth century: belief in the autonomy of the human reason and conscience, in the right of every person to the

---

15. *Ibid.*, p. 268.

maximum possible "happiness", in the nation-state as the entity to which one looks for the securing of these rights, and in the methods of modern science as the means for understanding and controlling events. Clearly all of these have been much modified and developed in the course of the past two hundred years. In particular the developments in modern physics, especially since Einstein, have destroyed the Newtonian picture of an "objective" world of matter in motion to which the observer is wholly external. But these new perspectives in science have not yet changed popular ways of thinking. The "public world" is still controlled by the ideas which came to vivid consciousness at the Enlightenment. Normally they are not called in question. They are the self-evident starting point for argument.

What is now being proposed is that not just in the private world but also in the public world another model for understanding is needed; that this in turn requires the acknowledgment that our most fundamental beliefs cannot be demonstrated but are held by faith; that it is the respon- sibility of the Church to offer this new model for understand- ing as the basis for a radical renewal of our culture; and that without such radical renewal our culture has no future. This is — if one may put it very sharply — an invitation to recover a proper acknowledgment of the role of dogma. It is an invitation to the Church to be bold in offering to the men and women of our culture a way of understanding which makes no claim to be demonstrable in the terms of "modern" thought, which is not "scientific" in the popular use of that word, which is based unashamedly on the revela- tion of God made in Jesus Christ and attested in scripture and the tradition of the Church, and which is offered as a fresh starting point for the exploration of the mystery of human existence and for coping with its practical tasks not only in the private and domestic life of the believers but also in the public life of the citizen.

IV. Three questions

At the close of the previous section I have stated in the sharpest form my belief that we are at a point in the history of the "modern" world at which the accepted framework of understanding has become inadequate and a new framework is called for. I have asked for an unembarrassed offering of the Christian "dogma" as that framework. In other words, I am asking for an authentically missionary approach to "modern" culture.

To state the matter thus is at once to invite three questions which must now be answered.

1. How is the proper role of dogma to be preserved from distortion into that attitude of mind which has made "dogmatism" a term of abuse?

2. If the Christian revelation is to be taken as the framework for understanding and action in the public sphere — in politics, economics and social organization — how can we avoid falling again into the "Constantinian" trap? From one point of view the Enlightenment was part of Europe's recoil from the horrible religious wars of the seventeenth century. Those wars marked the final break-up of the synthesis of Church, state and society which began with the baptism of the Emperor Constantine. Does my proposal amount to an invitation to return to the ideology of "Christendom"?

3. Does scripture in fact give us any authority for specifically Christian judgments and actions in the public sphere?

These questions have to be faced before the argument of this book can be carried further. The three are so interrelated that it is not possible entirely to separate the answers.

A. Dogma and dialogue

At the crucial point in my argument I have been following Polanyi, and I shall venture to quote him once again. The fundamental point which Polanyi makes is that knowing any reality is impossible except on the basis of some "framework" which is — in the act of knowing — uncriticized, and which cannot be demonstrated by reference to some more ultimate ground of belief. He writes:

> We must now recognize belief once more as the source of all knowledge. Tacit assent and intellectual passions, the sharing of an idiom and of a cultural heritage, affiliation to a like-minded community: such are the impulses which shape our vision of the nature of things on which we rely for our mastery of things. No intelligence, however critical or original, can operate outside such a fiduciary framework.[16]

The acknowledgment that this is so does not, however, mean that all questions are answered. The "fiduciary framework" is the starting point, not the cut-off point for exploration and questioning. Therefore (to quote again):

> The process of examining any topic is both an exploration of the topic and an exegesis of our fundamental beliefs in the light of which we approach it: a dialectical combination of exploration and exegesis. Our fundamental beliefs are continuously reconsidered in the course of such a process, but only within the scope of their own basic premises.[17]

So far I am following Polanyi. At this point, however, I think we have to take a further step which Polanyi does not take and which leads us on into the second question. In an earlier writing I suggested that the Christian mission has a logical structure analogous to that proposed by Polanyi in his account of knowing. I wrote:

> (The Christian mission) is an acting out of a fundamental belief and at the same time a process in which this belief is being constantly reconsidered in the light of the experience of acting it out in every sector of human affairs and in dialogue with every other pattern of thought by which men and women seek to make sense of their lives.[18]

Here a new factor is introduced, that of dialogue with other patterns of thought. No "fiduciary framework" or "pattern", in the sense that we are using these words, can exist except as it is held by a community. Science is the enterprise of a confraternity of scholars who share the same

---

16. *Ibid.*, p. 267.
17. *Ibid.*, p. 267.
18. *The Open Secret*, 1978, p. 31.

basic framework of thought; it would be impossible without this confraternity. Every such confraternity develops some of the characteristics of an "establishment" which exercises power. The scientific community, existing and operating internationally, is an extremely powerful establishment — perhaps the only one powerful enough to challenge the ideology of nationalism. Through the network of scientific publications this establishment determines what ideas qualify for circulation in the community and what do not. There are of course always some rebels, and there are marginal cases where it is uncertain whether or not a passport can be granted. The study of extra-sensory perception seems at times to have been in this position. But the point is that no systematic science is possible except where there is some kind of community which sustains and protects the "fiduciary framework" within which research and discussion are conducted. And every such community has power.

The "Constantinian" establishment effectively identified the Christian dogmatic framework with the supreme political power. In such a situation there is no room for dialogue. Deviation from the "fiduciary framework" means exclusion from the civil society. Europe has rightly rejected that synthesis which finally broke down in the religious wars of the seventeenth century. The Soviet Union has attempted to re-create it in another form, but it can only be sustained by the use of a kind of coercion against which the human spirit eternally rebels. Our modern western culture now acknowledges plurality as an irreversible fact. We recognize that different "fiduciary frameworks" co-exist and will continue to do so. The question is whether they are to co-exist merely in mutual toleration or in dialogue. Polanyi writes: "Our fundamental beliefs are continuously re-considered ... but only within the scope of their own basic premises." Dialogue, if it is genuine, takes us beyond this point to the place where we allow the "fiduciary framework" itself to be called in question.

This is not always recognized. There are many contemporary Christian exponents of the virtues of dialogue who make it clear in their writings that their "fiduciary framework" is safe from fundamental questioning. It may be some form of idealistic philosophy, a religious interpretation which can accommodate all religions, or the "scientific world-view", but the dialogue between religions and ideologies is conducted within this framework. It is, to quote a sharp Hindu observer, "dialogue insured against risk". In genuine dialogue it is the ultimate "fiduciary framework" which is put at risk, and there is therefore always the possibility of that radical "paradigm shift" which is called "conversion".

I hope it is now clear that in asking for a fresh recognition of the proper role of dogma, I am not asking that we should attempt to return to the middle ages. My proposal would be retrogressive and sterile if the plea for a proper acknowledgment of the role of dogma were not coupled with the requirement that we learn to live in real dialogue with those who operate from other "fiduciary frameworks". I do plead that the Church recognize with fresh clarity that it is the community entrusted with a "fiduciary framework" which offers a new starting point for understanding and coping with experience. As such a community it is necessarily a political and social fact, but it must never again aspire to the political and social power that the Constantinian establishment gave it. It must live in genuine and open dialogue with those who live by other "frameworks". But the supremely critical dialogue which it must now face is not the dialogue with other religions (important as that certainly is) but the dialogue with the culture which took its shape at the Enlightenment and with which the European churches have lived in an illegitimate syncretism ever since. Such a dialogue will always mean that our own basic presuppositions are called in question by the other party. Because of what I believe about Jesus Christ I believe that this open encounter can only lead both the Church and the other partners in the dialogue into a fuller apprehension of the truth. This is not "dialogue insured against risk"; it is part of the ultimate commitment of faith — a commitment which always means risking everything.

What I am pleading for is a genuinely missionary encounter with post-Enlightenment culture. We have too long accepted the position of a privileged option for the private sector. We have been tempted either to withdraw into an intellectual ghetto, seeking to preserve a kind of piety in church and home while leaving the public world (including the world of scholarship) to be governed by another ideology. Or we have been tempted to regard the "modern scientific world-view" as though it were simply a transcript of reality which we must — willy-nilly — accept as true. We then try to adjust our Christian beliefs to the requirements of "modern thought" and to find some room for ideas, sentiments and policies which are suggested to us by the Christian tradition — but always within the framework of the "modern scientific world-view". A truly missionary approach would reject both of these strategies; would recognize frankly the fact that the Christian dogma offers a "fiduciary framework" quite different from and (in some respects) incompatible with the framework within which modern European culture has developed; and would be quite bold and uncompromising in setting forth the Christian "dogma", but also very humble and teachable in engaging in dialogue with those who live by other fundamental beliefs.

B. No return to Constantine

In trying to answer the first question I have obviously started to open up the second. It is customary to speak of the conversion of Constantine (whether it was in fact genuine or "diplomatic") as one of the major disasters of Church history. This judgment is made today from within a culture which has almost completely removed Christianity from the public into the private sector. A little reflection will show the lack of realism behind this opinion.

The message of Jesus was about the kingship, the universal sovereignty of God. It was not a message about the interior life of the soul considered in abstraction from the public life of the world. The Church, therefore, was being faithful to the message of Jesus when it insisted that the claim of Jesus had priority over those of the Emperor. By this insistence the Church placed itself on a collision course with the imperial power. It would have been easy to avoid

That refusal to worship the emperor was
by implication more than a 'religious' act
is demonstrated it could be argued by
the triumph of the Church over the emperor.

the collision. Roman law distinguished between the "public cult" and the many "private cults" which flourished especially in the eastern part of the Empire. The former, centred in the worship of the Emperor, was seen as the bond holding society together. The latter embraced a great variety of societies which offered to their members ways of personal salvation through various disciplines and beliefs. There was a great variety of words to denote these religious societies. The opponents of Christianity used these words to refer to the Church, but no Christian of the first three centuries apparently ever did so. In other words, the Church did not regard itself as a society for the promotion of the personal salvation of its members. If it had been content to do so, it would have enjoyed the protection of the law — the same protection which churches enjoy in our modern culture, available for exactly the same reason — namely that they pose no threat to the ideology which controls public life. The early Church's Bible — the Greek Old Testament — had two words to denote the congregation of God's people. One of these — *sunagogos* — was already in current use to describe the Jewish communities existing as religious minorities throughout the Empire. The other — *ecclesia* — denoted the public assembly called from time to time by the civic authority, an assembly to which all citizens were summoned and in which the public affairs of the city were discussed and settled. By calling itself the *ecclesia Theou*, the ecclesia of God, the Church made its own self-understanding plain. It was the public assembly to which all humankind was summoned, which was called not by the town clerk but by God. In such an assembly, no earthly emperor could claim supremacy. But such a kind of assembling Roman law could not permit.

For two and a half centuries, with varying degrees of violence, the conflict between the two claims was fought out. From the side of the Church the hope was not for political success; it could not be. The hope was for the apocalypse of God's reign before which all rival claims would vanish away. The Church's only weapons were the word of testimony and the faithfulness of the martyrs — the witnesses. Those weapons proved in the end more powerful than the weapons held by the empire. That empire lost the will to resist, because the world-view on which it was founded proved inadequate. The classical world had come to the end of its spiritual resources. The thing which no earlier Christian could have dreamed of happened. The Emperor bowed his head to the yoke of Christ.

What, then, should the Church have done? Should it have advised the Emperor that it was better for the spiritual health of the Church, and therefore for the purpose of God, that he should remain a pagan and continue to persecute the Church? Let us forget — let us even forgive — the absurdities with which the Emperor was hailed as almost a second Christ. How else, at that moment of history, could the Church have expressed its faithfulness to the Gospel which is a message about the universal reign of God? It is hard to see what other possibility there was at that moment. The experiment of a Christian political order had to be made. It was made, and its fruits include the creation of "Christian Europe" out of which the modern world has been born. But the experiment ended in the hopeless strife of the religious wars. Europe, turning its back in weariness on the futile conflict, found a new "fiduciary framework" for its public life. We have already sketched its outlines. There is no way back to the Constantinian alliance between Church and state. We are now faced with a new task which may be defined as follows: how to embody in the life and teaching of the Church the claim that Christ is Lord over all life, without falling into the Constantinian impasse? The answering of that question will require decades of costly search and experiment, but a few basic guidelines can be sketched.

The mission of Jesus was to announce and embody the reign of God, a reign which claims jurisdiction over the whole created world and all that is in it. The conflict between that claim and the power that exercises usurped dominion in the world was fought and settled on the cross. The victory lies on the other side of death. Yet in the resurrection of Jesus and in the gift of the Spirit we have received now, in this age, a pledge and foretaste of that victory. The horizon of all our action in the world, therefore, is not an earthly utopia but the heavenly city which is God's new creation. The key to a right answering of our question lies in a true eschatology.

The Bible closes with a vision of the holy city coming down from heaven to earth. It is the vision of a consummation which embraces both the public and the private life of men and women. There is no dichotomy between these two. Those who die before that day are laid to rest in a "dormitory" around the church where the living continue to worship. When the Day comes, all together will share the same end — judgment and, for the blessed, the heavenly city.

The new framework which replaced the biblical one separated the public from the private vision. As far as public history is concerned, the human person — according to the new vision — is the bearer of history's purpose. Men and women themselves, with all the new powers that science gives, will create the heavenly city on earth. It is this expectation which gives meaning to public life. For the individual, there is a different hope. It is the hope of blessedness in another world to which you escape when death releases you from this one. From that point on, the future history of this world is not your concern. If you are (or were) a Protestant, you will not even be asked to go on praying for those who are still in the midst of the struggle. You have simply been removed from history.

The practical corollary of this vision is — of course — the privatization of religion. Churches become exactly what the early Church refused to be. They become privileged societies for the spiritual development of their members with a view to their ultimate blessedness in another world. The Church is no longer the *ecclesia Theou*; it is a congeries of *thiasoi*, of *heranoi*, religious fraternities offering consumer satisfaction to all kinds of people who are — of course — encouraged to "join the church of your choice". Today, two centuries later, the vision for public history has almost completely faded. We do not now believe in "progress". We read what the eighteenth century philosophers wrote about the heavenly city with sad amusement. And, since the kind of "salvation" which a privatized religion offers is much nearer to a Hindu than to the biblical model, it is natural that many young people are inclined to believe that they will find something better by going East.

If the churches are to escape from their long (and rather comfortable) domestication in the private sector and to reclaim the public sector for the Gospel without falling into the "Constantinian trap", what is required is a return to the biblical vision of the last things which must govern all our secular obedience. Those parts of the New Testament which are usually called "apocalyptic" have naturally seemed strange and uncouth to privatized churches, but they point us to the essential issues. They offer no basis for a doctrine of earthly progress. They do not encourage us to look for the establishment of justice and peace on earth as the result of our effort. They point rather to more and more terrible conflict. But beyond that they promise justice and peace as the gift of God. And they therefore call for a patience and endurance which can remain faithful to the end. They are — in fact — the projection on to the screen of future history of that pattern which Christians have learned from the life, death and resurrection of Jesus.

The message of Jesus was of the presence of the reign of God in the midst of history as the reality with which every human being must take account. The message was addressed to the nation. It concerned God's government of all nations and all creation. When it was rejected, Jesus did not follow the Zealots in seeking to establish God's reign by force. That road was to end in the tragedy of Masada where the last remnants of the freedom fighters took their own lives. Nor did he withdraw from public life and follow the Essenes into the desert to wait and pray for the kingdom. That road ends in the crumbling ruins of Qumran. What he did was to challenge the public life of the nation, at the place and time of its most passionate sensitivity, with a claim to kingship which was at the same time quite uncompromising and completely vulnerable. The claim was rejected and he was destroyed. But God raised him from the dead (an event in public history which our privatized religion has naturally converted into a purely psychological experience of the disciples) as the sign and pledge of the fact that the claim stands even though it is rejected by the world.

Christian discipleship is a following of Jesus in the power of his risen life on the way which he went. That way is neither the way of purely interior spiritual pilgrimage, nor is it the way of realpolitik for the creation of a new social order. It goes the way that Jesus went, right into the heart of the world's business and politics, with a claim which is both uncompromising and vulnerable. It looks for a world of justice and peace, not as the product of its own action but as the gift of God who raises the dead and "calls into existence the things that do not exist" (Rom. 4:17). It looks for the holy city not as the product of its policies but as the gift of God. Yet it knows that to seek escape from politics into a private spirituality would be to turn one's back on the true city. It looks for the city "whose builder and maker is God", but it knows that the road to the city goes down out of sight, the way Jesus went, into that dark valley where both our selves and all our works must disappear and be buried under the rubble of history. It therefore does not invest in any political programme (whether conceived in the style of a restored "Christendom" or in the style of a classless society where all coercive government will have withered away) the hopes and expectations which belong properly only to the city which God has promised. There can be no repetitions of Constantine, either on the left or on the right. What is required is a faithful discipleship, following Jesus on the road he went, and living by the hope of which his resurrection is the outward pledge and the gift of the Spirit the inward foretaste. Such discipleship will be concerned equally in the private and in the public spheres to make visible that understanding and ordering of life which takes as its "fiduciary framework" the revelation of himself which God has given in Jesus. It will provide occasions for the creation of visible signs of the invisible kingship of God.

C. Have we a mandate to "meddle in politics"?

My attempt to answer the second question has already led into the third. What are we to say to those many Christians like Dr Edward Norman for whom it seems obvious that

Christianity is "concerned primarily with the relationships of the soul to eternity",[19] and that Christians should therefore refrain from pretending that their Christian faith authorizes them to make judgments on political matters? The series of Reith Lectures from which that phrase is quoted was an eloquent exposition of that view, and it must be admitted that Dr Norman was justified in saying that much Christian speaking and writing on public issues has been based more on currently popular ideologies than on scripture and the Christian creeds. However, the sentence quoted above serves as a reminder of the fact that Dr Norman's religion is much nearer to the Upanishads than to the Bible. Yet views of this kind are widely shared by Christians who honestly believe that they are in fact holding the faith of the Bible and of the Church. What can be said on this beyond what I have already said? Recognizing the complexity of the issues involved, I venture to offer the following for consideration.

(1) The division of the human person into "soul" and "body" is a reversion to the ancient pagan dichotomy from which the biblical vision delivered the classical world. Nothing is more striking than the contrast at this point between the Bible and the main lines of Indian thought. Indian religion is an enormously complex world of experience, thought and practice, but one very pervasive theme has been the relative unreality of the "public" world. Corresponding to this has been the belief that the essence of the human person is to be discovered by stripping away those aspects of our human nature which connect us with the world of nature and the world of other people. In a famous passage of the Taitiriya Upanishad, for example, it is taught that in order to find the real person one must go behind the material ("food"), the vital ("breath"), the intellectual ("mind") and the spiritual ("understanding").[20] The real person, the ultimate self, is hidden behind all these. This is the "soul" which, as in Dr Norman's world-view, is directly

---

19. *Christianity and World Order*, 1979, p. 80.
20. *Taitiriya Upanishad*, II 1-5.

related to eternity. When one turns to the Bible one finds nothing at all of this attempt to locate the real person behind all these contingent elements. On the contrary, the human person is defined from the beginning in terms of the mutuality of male and female, and in terms of the mutual responsibilities of the members of a family, and of families and nations to each other. There is no dichotomy between the inward and the outward aspects of human beings. The dichotomy of "soul" and "body" is foreign to the biblical world-view. And this corresponds to normal healthy human experience, for we do not become persons at all except as we share in a common life with other human persons within and depending on the life of nature. It is of course true that while we see ourselves from within, others see us and we see others from without. But these two complementary ways of seeing human nature do not amount to a division of the human person into two separate entities.

The kingship of God, present in Jesus, concerns the whole of human life in its public as well as its private aspects. There is no basis in scripture for the withdrawal of the public aspect of human life from that obedience which the disciple owes to the Lord. The question, therefore, is not: "What grounds can be shown for Christian involvement in public life?" It is: "What grounds can be shown for the proposal to withdraw from the rule of Christ the public aspects of our human living?" The answer is: "None."

(2) The matter is, however, more serious than the above formulation suggests. The truth is that, in those areas of our human living which we do not submit to the rule of Christ, we do not remain free to make our own decisions: we fall under another power. We become, in Pauline language, slaves to the "principalities and powers", to the "elemental spirits of the universe" (Gal. 4:3). Paul used this language in addressing Christians who thought that their obedience to Christ was something falling within their obedience to the Mosaic law, rather than something transcending it. Against this Paul insists that the law was a good gift of God but that if it did not yield place to Christ it became a power to enslave. Paul has much to say in several letters about these

"principalities and powers". They are the "rulers of this world" who did not recognize the kingship of Christ, who sought to destroy him, and who were themselves robbed of their absolute power — not destroyed but "disarmed" (1 Cor. 2:8, Col. 1:20). They have been created in Christ and for Christ (Col. 1:16) and they have a good purpose (Rom. 13:1). They prepare the way for Christ (Gal. 3:24, Rom. 8:20f.). But when they fail to acknowledge the absolute sovereignty of Christ and claim absolute sovereignty themselves, they become instruments of the evil one. So the Law, which is God's gift, becomes a yoke of bondage. So the imperial power, which was given by God for the maintenance of justice, becomes an embodiment of demonic evil (cf. Rom. 13 and Rev. 13).[21]

We have had terrible examples of what Paul is describing in the history of our own culture. When, at the birth of our modern world, economics came to be regarded as no longer part of ethics but as an autonomous science governed by immanent laws to be discovered by analysis and induction, and when this new faith was embodied in the myth of the "invisible hand" which could ensure that the sum total of individual self-seeking would add up to general welfare, good Christians contemplating the appalling cruelties of the "dark Satanic mills" believed that it was impossible to interfere with the workings of "economic laws", that the writ of Christ's kingship did not run in the autonomous kingdom of economics, and that the best one could do was to offer charity to the victims. Blake was correctly interpreting the biblical teaching when he used the word "Satanic" at this point. Any sphere of human life which is withdrawn from the kingship of Christ does not remain under ours; it falls under another rule.

An even more contemporary example is to be found in South Africa today. The doctrine of apartheid owes its origin in part to the teaching of missionaries who wished to cherish the cultural values of the African peoples and to avoid forcing them into the mould of European culture.

---

21. For a classical treatment of this theme, see H. Berkhof, *Christ and the Powers*, ET 1962, Herald Press, Scottdale, Pa.

They were acknowledging the good gift of God in those bonds of family, language and culture which give us so much of our human identity. But when race was absolutized and treated as an unchanging part of creation within and under which the saving work of Christ is to be received, then what was good became an instrument of Satanic evil.

The decision for Christians is not whether or not to become involved as Christians in public affairs. It is whether our responsibilities in the public sphere are to be discharged under the kingship of Christ or under the dominion of the evil one.

(3) But what is meant by "Christian involvement in public affairs"? Here a vast range of difficult questions appears.

(a) A distinction has to be made between the activities of individual Christians, and the actions and pronouncements of the Church as an organized body functioning through its official representatives — whether a hierarchy or a synod. The sharpness of this distinction varies in accordance with the extent to which the Church is so organized that its entire lay membership has a significant role in the making of official decisions. In the end, the witness of the Church in respect of public issues will depend more upon the day-to-day behaviour of its members than on its official words and actions. A church, acting officially in its corporate capacity, may decide to speak or not to speak on a public issue, but the Church is in any case involved in these issues because its members are citizens, workers, employers, teachers, writers, buyers and sellers — members of society whose words and behaviour are constantly shaping public life in one direction or another. From this there is no possibility of withdrawal. For them the question is whether their judgments, and therefore their words and actions in the public sphere, are governed by the reigning assumptions of society or by their Christian obedience. A church acting corporately is probably wise to confine its official pronouncements on public questions to a limited range of matters where great ethical issues are at stake. But the Church must be constantly assisting its members to form their judgment upon these matters in the light of their faith. Those who are responsible for teaching and for pastoral leadership in the Church are failing in their duty if they do not try to do this.

(b) It is generally agreed that Christians cannot completely identify any particular political programme with obedience to the will of God revealed in Christ. The introduction of absolutes into politics is always disastrous. A sober doctrine of human sinfulness will prevent us from investing in particular political programmes the hopes which belong properly only to the last things. Yet it would be wrong to move from this proper sense of the fallibility of all human judgments to a complete relativism, to a political twilight in which all cats are grey, to conclude — for example — that there is nothing to choose from a Christian point of view between Julius Nyerere's Tanzania and Franco's Spain.[22] It was one of the very great gifts of Reinhold Niebuhr that he could illuminate both the disastrous consequences of introducing a Christian absolute into politics, and at the same time the absolute obligation of Christians to discern the relative less or more of justice and freedom, and to commit themselves to action on behalf of that which was relatively better.

(c) There will always be among Christians different opinions, different discernments, different commitments among the relativities of politics. But on this two things have to be said.

(i) The differences have to be subject to continuous and vigorous discussion. They concern matters of right and wrong, of obedience and disobedience. They are not matters of taste on which we can simply agree to differ. Even while we accept one another in Christ as fellow-sinners redeemed by grace, we are also under obligation to seek to convince one another about what we believe obedience to Christ requires in the public sphere. This continuous effort of mutual persuasion and correction about public duty is a necessary part of the ongoing life of the Church.

(ii) There is not, however, an unlimited field for choice. There can be options in the field of public life which the Church as a whole must judge to be heretical, incompatible

---

22. E. Norman, *op. cit.*, p. 81.

with Christian discipleship. The acquiescence of the official German churches in the racial policies of the Nazis, and the support of the white Dutch Reformed churches for the racial policies of the present South African government have been widely regarded as examples of positions which the Church cannot acknowledge as consistent with Christian discipleship. There may be others. An international economic order, for example, which works steadily and inexorably to divide the world into a rich sector which expects to become richer with each year that passes, and a poor sector which sinks ever deeper into poverty, is in flagrant contradiction to the will of God as revealed in Christ. There can be legitimate differences of opinion about alternative possibilities for the ordering of the economic life of the nations, but when the cause of Christianity is identified with the resolute defence of the existing capitalist structure, if necessary by the use of nuclear weapons, then the question about the limits of permissible diversity, the question of apostasy, has to be raised.

(4) There is a quite different set of difficulties which arises from the present position of biblical scholarship after two centuries in which the critical study of the Bible has been conducted mainly within the "fiduciary framework" of the Enlightenment. Basic to this approach, as we have seen, was the shift from an "explanation" which took revelation as the starting point to an "explanation" based on the observation and analysis of observable facts with a view to discovering their "laws", that is their necessary relations. This "framework" required that the text of scripture be examined on the same basis as any other text in the total corpus of ancient literature. The labour of generations of scholars working on this basis has shown that the scriptures as we have them are the end-product of a very long process of collecting, editing and rewriting oral and written traditional material, all arising from and dependent on the various cultures of western Asia during a period of more than a thousand years.

The consequence is that it has become very difficult for a person who is part of modern western culture to treat the

Bible as an authoritative guide for conduct — whether in the private or in the public sphere. Several distinct issues are involved here. Firstly, modern historical scholarship has brought to light the cultural remoteness of the worlds in and for which the texts were originally written. This makes it difficult for the modern reader to see how they are applicable to the twentieth century world. Secondly, scholarship has shown that the scriptures as we have them are the result of combining materials which in their original form represented quite different and even contradictory beliefs. An obvious example is the juxtaposition of two apparently quite contrary assessments of kingship in the first Book of Samuel. On almost every contemporary ethical issue it is possible to find in scripture texts which support mutually contrary decisions.

Appeals to scripture on the basis of isolated texts are rightly condemned, but the only alternative — unless we are to abandon any reliance upon the authority of scripture — is to take seriously the fact of the canon as both authorizing and limiting the diversity which scripture contains. This means that scriptural interpretation requires us to press beyond textual, literary, historical, form and redaction-criticism to an examination of the way in which the text relates to the canon as a whole. This discipline of "canonical criticism", which is being developed by biblical scholars in the USA, seems to hold real promise for the Church's continuing task of interpretation.

But any appeal to biblical authority raises questions which go to the heart of the debate with "modern" culture. The scriptures are written in faith and to evoke faith. They are concerned with answers to the most fundamental questions about the origin, meaning and goal of human life. A kind of scholarly examination which pretends to be neutral on these matters is incapable of interpreting the text in its original intention — namely to evoke faith. The scholar examines the text, but is not himself examined. His neutrality is already a decision against the faith which the text intends to evoke.

In fact, such a claim to neutrality would be false. The scholar comes to the text with the assumptions of the modern scientific world. The decisions about what questions are to be asked, and what tools are to be used in answering them, arise from that world. In the nineteenth century, the analytical methods of critical scholarship were used with brilliant effect to break up the material of the Pentateuch into the smallest possible units and then to recombine them in a frame shaped by the contemporary ideas of evolution and progress. This programme was carried through with genuine evangelistic zeal; the old view was to be replaced by a new one which would make the biblical story acceptable to modern people. But it is easy to see that there was no neutrality.

No scholarly activity is disinterested. It intends to serve some purpose. This applies as much to the study of biblical texts as to any other study. The biblical writers were in many cases interpreting earlier texts, and their interest is clear to the modern interpreter who examines their interpretation from his point of view. The black preacher in an inner-city congregation is engaged in interpreting texts in the interest of evoking faith in a God who liberates the oppressed and reconciles the estranged. The interpretation is not a disinterested one, and the preacher does not pretend to be neutral. Biblical scholars on university faculties are likewise interested people. They may share the interest of the preacher, as many of the greatest scholars do. They may also have an interest in securing the approval of the academic world, without which their work will not be made available to others through publication. This interest will govern the questions they take up for study and the methods they use in probing them. They may be honestly seeking assured and reliable conclusions, but they presumably also know that the principles of their science call for the unremitting application of criticism to all alleged conclusions, and that their "assured results" will certainly be questioned and replaced in a few years. But meanwhile the scholars are part of an institution which measures success in the terms which are set by our culture and they themselves have a clear interest in achieving success in these terms — by the publication of their work and by advancement in the academic world. Their interest is as manifest as that of the preacher.

But which interest is the key to the understanding of scripture? Here no neutral stance is possible. One cannot commend an appeal to the authority of the Bible by "proving" its truth or reliability to modern man and woman, for that proof would have to rest upon the very assumptions which the Bible calls in question. It is, of course, both possible and legitimate to interpret the Bible from the perspective of our culture, just as it is possible and legitimate for a Hindu, a Muslim or a Marxist to interpret it from these other perspectives. The Church can and must learn from all of these. But the Church is that community which, in an unbroken succession from Abraham, lives by the faith to which the Bible bears witness, and continues to testify in face of all other claims that it is in this faith that the truth is to be known in its fullness. That is an ultimate faith-commitment; it cannot be validated by reference to something else presumed to be more reliable. The Church's interpretation of the scriptures is within a commitment to faith and obedience such that, while each generation must seek to understand them in its own terms, the scriptures constantly call these terms in question. The scriptures can never be, for the Church, a collection of texts from the past which can be studied "objectively" by a scholar who remains uncommitted to their truth. The Church, in exposing itself constantly to the words of the scripture, finds itself questioned, its own assumptions challenged, its ways of understanding changed. The understanding of scripture in the Church has to be in this context of faith, openness and obedience. The only proper "interest" of the Church in the study of scripture is the glory of the one who speaks to the Church in scripture.

But meanwhile, although the Church has never ceased to cherish the scriptures in its worship and private devotion, there is real diffidence about any appeal to scripture as an authoritative source of guidance for conduct in public affairs. Many Christians feel themselves to be in a position analogous to that which was a ground of complaint at the time of the Reformation. At that time the complaint was that the Bible had been taken out of the hands of the laity and become the property of the clergy. Now it has to be asked whether it has not become the property of the guild of scholars in such a way that the ordinary lay person feels unable to understand it without the help of a trained expert.

But the lay person knows also that the results of modern critical scholarship are by their nature ephemeral. The critical method systematically devours its products. Even the well-instructed lay person is therefore always left in doubt about whether what he or she has been told may not be already out of date.

Yet it must be said plainly that there is no way by which the Bible can be restored to the laity by taking it out of the hands of the scholars. The results of two centuries of critical study cannot be wished away. And the layman and woman are themselves part of modern culture and cannot with integrity divide their mental world into two parts, one controlled by that culture and the other by the Bible. A much more exciting and costly move is called for, namely a genuinely missionary encounter between a scriptural faith and modern culture. By this I mean an encounter which takes our culture seriously yet does not take it as the final truth by which scripture is to be evaluated, but rather holds up the modern world to the mirror of the Bible in order to understand how we, who are part of modern culture, are required to re-examine our assumptions and reorder our thinking and acting. This is, I believe, our present task.

The Church has never ceased to place the scriptures in the centre of its life. In doing so, it continues to bear witness to a "fiduciary framework" different from and older than that of our culture. What would it mean to confront the axioms and assumptions of our culture with those of the Bible? At the risk of superficiality in a field where large and complex issues are being intensively discussed by philosophers, theologians and biblical scholars, let me venture briefly to suggest the following guidelines for such a missionary encounter.[23]

(a) There is no way by which the Bible can be insulated from what Walter Lippmann called the "acids of moder-

---

23. In what follows I am much indebted to Paul Ricoeur, *Essays in Biblical Interpretation*.

nity", exempted from the kind of critical analysis to which Enlightenment culture has subjected all experience. Nor should we wish that it should be otherwise. We shall have to draw attention to the limitations which necessarily belong to this kind of analysis, but as long as we accept its validity for the rest of our experience, we cannot deny it access to the Bible without removing the latter from the real world to a world of make-believe. In a proper concern to be faithful to the fundamentals of the Christian faith, it is easy to be trapped into a fundamentalism which treats the scriptures as a "scientific" account of the things recorded. This is itself a typically "Enlightenment" approach: the autonomous reason dealing with "objective" facts from the past. When, for example, the creation sagas of Genesis are presumed to be statements of the same order as Darwin's "Origin of Species", so that a choice has to be made between the two, the scriptures are being read through spectacles provided by the Enlightenment. This kind of "fundamentalism" is a product of modern culture, and its representatives find it easy to be very much at home in the modern world and to prosper on the terms which the modern world offers. It is something quite different from the pre-critical attitude of those who have never been exposed to the "acids of modernity" and read the scriptures quite naturally as part of their own world.

(b) Scripture, like every other text, must be allowed to speak for itself. It must not be forced to speak in other categories than its own. This is what happens when scripture is reduced to a series of doctrinal statements. When we actually attend to scripture we hear a great many voices and they use different forms of speech. In prophecy there is a human voice which speaks the divine word of promise and warning at a particular time to a specific situation. In narrative a voice, usually anonymous, tells of events in which God has acted and so made his intention known. In the instruction of *Torah* God is leading the redeemed people to an ever more personal and inward grasping of that intention. In the wisdom literature there is an address to every human being about how right conduct is related to the ultimate constitution of things. And in the psalms and hymns we hear

Oddly he leaves out the hugely important 586 Exile parallel to the crucifixion. Return and Resurrection.

the voice of the redeemed community in praise, thanksgiving and supplication to God who is the author of prophecy, the actor in history and the source of instruction and wisdom. These different voices speak in their own different ways, and must be heard as they speak. They must not be synthesized into a series of propositions which can be solidified as "revealed truth" to be set against the kind of knowledge which is available through the study of nature and its laws.

(c) In what way, then, does scripture function as the bearer of revelation? I have emphasized its variety, and it goes without saying that modern scholarship has brought to light an immensely complex network of different strands within each of these elements. It has uncovered the many different sources from which material has been drawn, and the social, cultural, religious, political and economic interests which have played a part in shaping it. Yet the Bible comes to us in its "canonical shape", the result of many centuries of interpretation and reinterpretation, editing and re-editing, with a unity which depends upon certain discernible centres. These are events, happenings in the contingent world of history, which are interpreted as disclosures in a unique sense, of the presence and action of God. Essentially there are two primary centres — the rescue of Israel from Egypt, and the events concerning the man Jesus of Nazareth. The former provides the interpretative centre for the manifold and diverse material of the Old Testament; the latter provides the centre for the (likewise) very diverse material of the New. And the latter draws into its field the earlier centre, so that the events concerning Jesus are portrayed as the ultimate interpretation of the events concerning the Exodus.

These events are, from the beginning, interpreted events (as are, indeed, all the "facts of history"). They are interpreted as divine actions, as the presence of the absolute among the contingent events of history. But the interpretation has to be reinterpreted over and over again in terms of another generation and another culture. We see this process going on through all the layers of biblical material. The original interpretative language becomes a text which in turn needs interpretation, and so on till the end of time. It is never enough just to repeat the text.

Yet the text cannot be eliminated. The events are not mere symbols of an underlying reality which could be grasped apart from them. If that were the case, we would be dealing with mental concepts as ultimate and historical happenings as illustrative. Nor, again, are the events merely examples of a general rule which can be formulated apart from them. All such attempts to translate the events into symbols or examples of a timeless truth which can be embodied in propositional statements, are opposed to the essential nature of what is presented in the Bible as *testimony*.

(d) Testimony, or witness, is a kind of utterance different from the statement of a fact which is self-evident or can be demonstrated from self-evident premises. It is not a logically inescapable "truth of reason". A witness makes his or her statement as part of a trial in which the truth is at stake, in which the question: "What is the truth?" is being argued; it is not, while the trial proceeds, presumed to be already common knowledge. Throughout the Bible, the statements made about the great events of exodus and atonement have the character of witness. They are made in the context of contestation. The witness stakes his or her being and life on a statement which can be contradicted. It is, of course, a statement of fact and meaning in indissoluble unity, and it is made in face of the powers that deny it — the "idols", the "ruler of this world". The final proof of the statement will not be available until the trial is over and the judge has pronounced the verdict. To ask for another kind of "proof" is to show that one has not understood what is going on.

(e) What is the content of the testimony? Essentially it is a witness to the living God traces of whose presence and action have been granted in the events which are recounted. They are "traces". God cannot be enclosed in any statement we make or any vision we have. To the question: "What is your name?", the answer is: "I will be who I will be" (Ex. 3:14). It is not "I am what I am", a translation based on the Greek rendering of the Exodus story which could too easily replace the living God of the Bible by the "Absolute", or "Transcendent Being" — a concept which the mind is capable of formulating out of the processes of thought itself. We are concerned with a real meeting, an encounter with another, not with a part of the furniture of the thinking mind. The living God goes before us, but also comes to meet us, and there are witnesses who can testify that God has called them to follow. We are not dealing with an idea among the ideas which we can conceive out of the processes of our own thought. We are dealing with one who meets and summons us in events which form part of history, events which invite us to trust the promise of one whom now we cannot see face to face, but who goes before us with a presence which is also a promise.

This pattern is confirmed in the New Testament. The living God was present in the man Jesus, but to understand the truth in its fullness is not given even to his closest disciples there and then; it will be made known to them by the living Spirit of God as they follow him on the way of the cross and become bearers of his testimony.

(f) This testimony has to be given now, as always, in the midst of a trial in which it is contested. The culture of which we are a part has prized above all the autonomy of reason. For this culture the witness of scripture is offensive in two ways.

(i) Our culture is offended by the idea that the Absolute should be made known in contingent happenings of history. It has become almost an axiom that "the accidental truths of history can never become the proof of necessary truths of reason" (Lessing). According to the ruling assumptions of our culture, human reason in its autonomy has direct access to truth; accidental happenings of history may illustrate this truth but can never prove it. To say that "God was in Christ", or to repeat the word attributed to Jesus, "I am the Way", is to challenge these assumptions. It is to make human reason dependent for contact with ultimate truth upon one particular happening among all the accidental happenings of history. To say that the transcendent is to be truly known only by looking at one particular series of events with all their particularity of time, place, race, culture and language, is to pose a direct challenge to the sovereignty of the autonomous reason as our culture has prized it.

(ii) This challenge is doubly offensive because it appears like the invasion of an alien power which menaces the freedom of enquiry and conscience. Let us at once confess that Christians have compounded the problem by misrepresenting divine revelation as a body of "truths" which can be fully encapsulated in a series of doctrinal statements guaranteed by the authority of the Church. The Enlightenment was in part a legitimate and proper revolt against an authority wrongly claimed in the name of revelation. The battle which was fought by those of the Enlightenment, and by the pioneers of modern science, for freedom of conscience and freedom of enquiry, was one in which Christians were often on the wrong side. This must be acknowledged. But having made this acknowledgment, we must not allow earlier errors to prevent us from giving the testimony which we are bound to give. Our culture rests upon an illusion. Human reason and conscience are not autonomous. The human spirit is not sovereign of the world it perceives. The way of understanding and managing the world which modern science has pursued with such dazzling success, is not the only way of understanding and managing, and by itself can only lead to death. There are vast reaches of experience which are only available to us when we are willing to open our hearts and imaginations to the appeal of beauty, to the deep sense of our kinship with nature and — above all — to the appeal of love. Such experience is experience of reality, and it is only available as we surrender our wills freely to a reality beyond ourselves. Because we are part of the whole fabric of created things, that appeal can only come to us through created things and contingent happenings. And it can come to us only as meaning, as interpreted happening. In this sense our reason and conscience have an inalienable responsibility for understanding, but it is part of the tragedy of the human self turned in upon itself that responsibility is construed as autonomy. Then the self, in the illusion of its autonomy, perceives the claim of revelation in particular happenings as a threat and an invasion. But the testimony which the Church has to give is of a revelation which is not an alien invasion threatening the freedom of the human spirit, but the appeal of a love which alone can set the human spirit free.

(g) But it remains testimony, not coercive proof. And (let it be said again) the context is a trial in which the witness has to stake his or her life on a truth which will not be demonstrated until the end. If the Church is bold in giving its testimony to the living God who is revealed in particular events and in the scriptures which are the primal witness to these events, then it must necessarily clash with our contemporary culture. It must challenge the whole "fiduciary framework" within which our culture operates. It must call unequivocally for radical conversion, a conversion of the mind so that things are seen differently, and a conversion of the will so that things are done differently. It must decline altogether the futile attempt to commend the biblical vision of how things are by seeking to adjust it to the assumptions of our culture.

(h) Yet the Church cannot give this testimony by simply repeating the words of the Bible. As in the scriptures themselves, and as in every subsequent age and every culture, so now in this age and culture the effort must be made to interpret the text in the language and thought-forms of our culture. This is always a risky undertaking, because the original testimony may be lost in the interpretation. It is easy to show how the figure of Jesus has been represented in one culture after another as merely an image of its own ideal. A gallery of the portraits of Jesus painted through the centuries tells us more about the minds of the painters than about Jesus. How can given revelation in the once-for-all events of which the Bible speaks be rendered authentically into the terms of a culture in such a way that there is a real encounter? The answer to that question can only be given in terms of the work of the Holy Spirit who is promised to the Church when it is willing to suffer for the sake of the testimony (e.g. Mark 13:11). The Spirit is the one whose witness makes possible the witness of the Church (John 15:18-27). The Spirit is the prosecutor who brings the fundamental axioms of a culture under judgment (John 16:7-11). The Spirit's presence is promised to the Church as a whole, and one of the implications of this is that we can only make our testimony effectively when we do it together with those whose culture is different from ours.

(i) The promise of the Holy Spirit to the Church is linked in the Gospels with the warning of conflict. The context is the trial in which truth is at stake. The promise is given to the Church which is faithful under trial. A missionary encounter with our culture will not be a matter of words only. It will entail actions which bring conflict and suffering. It would be unrealistic to think otherwise. The "fiduciary framework" which the Church has to offer in place of the one which has shaped and controlled our culture has its centre and source (as we have seen) in an appeal of love which can only be answered in faith, love and obedience. It is not just a matter of seeing "how things are" in a new light; it is also a matter of seeing what is to be done in this light. The kind of "understanding" which arises from accepting the testimony is not only a way of seeing; it is also a way of acting and expecting. It is a kind of knowing which consists in faith, hope and love: faith which risks everything on a testimony whose truth will only be proved at the end; hope which is always pressing forward confidently to that end; and love which is an overflow of life released from bondage to the self by the work of God in Christ, and which leads to actions which bear the authentic sign of the cross where that work of God has its centre.

V. An invitation to explore

The argument of this essay has been open to critical question at almost every point. I am trying to express a conviction which needs testing by abler minds working in many different disciplines. I have written in the hope of eliciting such questioning and testing because I believe that my main thesis is true even if inadequately stated. If it is true, then a new initiative is needed by the churches. It will not be enough to propose "Christian solutions" to the problems of our society, because it is the whole framework in which these "problems" are perceived which has to be called in question. Recent efforts by the British churches, such as those documented in *Britain Today and Tomorrow*, have been criticized on the ground that the proposals made depend more upon contemporary liberal opinion than upon exegesis of scripture and the Christian tradition. It seems that a more radical move is needed, a move which will involve calling in question some of the assumptions which our culture takes as "self-evident". It is natural that the Church should offer its message and its fellowship as the answer to the aspirations and hopes of men and women. But it has to be asked whether such an offer can be made, whether in fact the expectations of people today are not such that they are incapable of realization. It has to be asked whether the "revolution of expectations" which has been such an outstanding feature of the modern world is not a revolution doomed to disappointment because it is founded on illusion.

Clearly there is no single set of principles to be drawn from scripture and applied to modern society. To think so would be to repeat the old misunderstanding of revelation. It is a matter of becoming a witness in the midst of contemporary society to the action of the living God made known in the saving events which are narrated and interpreted in scripture. It is a matter of living in the expectation and hope which God's action makes possible now. We cannot expect all Christians to agree about exactly what is to be done in complex and changing situations. But we can indicate areas where a resolute challenge to the assumptions of our culture is called for. I want to suggest, by way of example, five such areas, in the hope that exploration by those competent in these areas would lead to decisions about how the situation is to be understood and what is to be said and done.

(a) A first area will be the understanding of what it means to be a human person. The Enlightenment saw the human person as an autonomous centre of knowing and judging in such wise that any sort of heteronomy was to be rejected. The implication of this view is that each person has the right to develop his or her own potential to the maximum, limited only by the parallel rights of other persons. The governing principle, therefore, will be that of equality, since every person has equal rights. Equality will mean that — ideally — each one will have all that is needed for personal development, and each one will be the judge of what those needs are. Dependence of one upon another is — in this view — incompatible with human dignity.

The biblical vision of the human person is different at every point. In this vision there is no true humanity without relatedness, which means that mutual dependence is intrinsic to true humanity. The governing principle, therefore, is not equality but mutuality — "one-anotherness", if one may create a noun out of Paul's constant reference to the duties we owe one another. The image of God in the human person is bound up with this mutual inter-relatedness and interdependence as man and woman (Gen. 1:27). There is no being human except in relatedness, and the true relation between human beings is expressed in the phrase: "Be servants one of another." In this vision, human persons find their dignity when they surrender their autonomy to one another, and lose it when they place their "equal rights" at the centre. And the centre which holds the whole "frame" together is the God who enters into a covenant of faithfulness with men and women created to mirror divine faithfulness by their faithful relatedness to one another.

We would have to ask what the implications of this vision would be for our economic systems. Both the major rival economic philosophies — of the world which calls itself "free" and the world which calls itself "socialist" — are founded upon the Enlightenment vision of the human person. Both are in deep trouble. Both make promises which they cannot fulfill. Is it possible to adumbrate a completely different vision of the ordering of economic life governed by the biblical vision of the human person? There have been notable essays in this direction. Is it not now time to make a bigger effort to spell out what this would imply?

(b) A second area of questioning will be about the goal of human life. Our culture has generally accepted as self-evident that the "pursuit of happiness" is the proper goal of any person. Against this assumption we have to bear witness to a different understanding of happiness. Happiness, in the biblical vision, is a gift of God, not a human achievement. The most famous passage in the Bible on the subject (Matt. 5: 3-11) promises happiness to those whom most people today would count most wretched. Yet there is a growing recognition among "modern" peoples, especially among the young, that the "happiness" so insistently offered by the advertising media in a consumer-oriented society is not happiness at all; that human dignity is not secured but lost in the plethora of "good things" which modern technology makes available.

In a world where only a small minority have access to this wealth, and where the majority still wage a desperate struggle for existence, there can be more than a little hypocrisy in the questioning of western affluence by those who enjoy it. But worse than hypocrisy is the futility of imagining that "development" for the whole human race can consist in enabling the rest of the world to catch up with the affluent minority. If the herd is rushing down the steep slope into the abyss, perhaps the laggards are to be congratulated!

We would have to ask — rich and poor together — what are the models of world development, rooted in the mutual responsibility of all, which will safeguard real human dignity, freeing ourselves completely from the illusion that "happiness" in the form that "modern" societies have sought it can ever be the goal of human living and the mark of human dignity. Development, so understood, will require more difficult changes for the rich world than for the poor.

(c) A third area of questioning will be about the capabilities and rights of governments. The founding fathers of the United States of America, having severed the bonds (however tenuous) which had connected them with the old kingship, and having therefore no transcendent authority which would legitimize the government they established, sought a kind of transcendent legitimation in "self-evident" truths which are not a matter of opinion but were binding upon all. (Hannah Arendt has suggested that they slipped when they used the first person plural pronoun. Strictly speaking it should have read: "These truths are self-evident." Personal opinion was not quite eliminated!) Among the truths held to be self-evident was the role of government in securing the rights of every person to life, liberty and the pursuit of happiness. Those of the French Revolution (in contrast to the Americans) found not transcendent authority but overwhelming power in the "general will of the people" — a will which, since it was never single and never constant, had to be challenged eventually through a single dictator. The nineteenth and twentieth centuries have seen an enormous expansion of the role of national governments in responding to the universal desire for life, liberty and happiness. The emphasis has fallen upon equal rights rather than upon mutual obligations, and the "self-evident" opinion that it is the duty of governments to implement these rights has led people everywhere to load upon their governments responsibilities for human happiness which no government in previous ages was expected to carry. Governments have come to be seen as the source from which all blessings flow, and because no government can deliver what is expected of it, cynicism follows.

Cynicism leads easily to the kind of reaction against state-supported welfare schemes which is at present apparent in Britain, for example, a reaction which in effect pampers the rich at the expense of the poor. Cynicism is sterile. We have to seek ways of expressing the mutual responsibility which all must share for the welfare of all in a more personal and face-to-face manner than is possible within the inevitable bureaucratic constraints of state-organized welfare. The search would require the expert guidance of those who have practical experience in the fields of welfare administration. There are very complex issues involved in the interlocking roles of national and local governments and voluntary bodies. It would only be fruitful if the vision which informed it all was a vision of human dignity not derived from the Enlightenment but from the Bible, a vision of human life in terms of mutual responsibilities rather than of equal rights, and of happiness not as a "right" but as a gift which is chiefly characterized by the fact that it surprises us when we are not looking for it.

(d) A fourth area of questioning will be about our vision of the future. The Enlightenment gave birth to the hope of an earthly utopia to be achieved by the liberation of reason and conscience from the shackles of dogma, and by the application of the scientific method to the exploitation of nature and the ordering of society. The liberal vision of gradual progress, a vision which was present even through the first decades of the twentieth century, has now completely faded. The hope of a utopia to be achieved by violent revolution is still alive among a small minority. The vast majority have, it seems, ceased to think hopefully about any earthly future. But without hope action is impossible and life ceases.

If we are controlled by the biblical vision, our hope for the future will be both firm and realistic. The apocalyptic writings of the New Testament offer — as I have said — a view of the future controlled by the events of the life, death and resurrection of Jesus. (There is a closer verbal parallel between the passion predictions and the apocalyptic passages in the Synoptic Gospels: in both cases "these things must come to pass"). The vision offered is not one of gradual progress. It is of deepening conflict, of the destruction of what seemed stable, and of a final victory beyond the darkness. The conflict is precipitated by the appearing of "false messiahs" — those, in other words, who pretend to offer total welfare on terms other than those which are offered to those who follow Jesus on the way of the cross. "Total welfare", freedom from all earthly ills as a this-worldly possibility, is an idea which could only arise within a culture which was familiar with the gospel announcement that the day of salvation has dawned. The coming of the true Messiah precipitates the appearing of the false ones. The secular promise of total welfare apart from discipleship in the way of the cross has been made and could only have been made from within a society shaped by the gospel. The promise is false and can only lead to disaster. The vision of the shape of things to come which the New Testament gives should enable Christians to be both realistic and hopeful, both eager and patient. The final victory of Jesus is assured, but it lies beyond the death and dissolution of both our persons and our societies. The actions that we take, therefore, will not be those which fear dictates; rather they will have the character of signs — like the action of the imprisoned Jeremiah buying a plot of land in enemy-held territory. They will be signs of hope. But the hope is not just for personal salvation; it is for the accomplishment of God's whole purpose in nature and history, and therefore the actions will be actions in the public as well as in the private sphere.

(e) And, finally, a fifth area of questioning will concern contemporary assumptions about what is involved in knowing. This is our most fundamental task, because the ways of knowing developed by modern science since the seventeenth century are fundamental to the whole of western culture. The greatest intellectual task facing the Church is a new dialogue with science— a dialogue for which the way has been prepared by profound changes in science (especially in physics) during this century. In an earlier chapter, quoting Michael Polanyi, I have indicated the way in which I believe this dialogue must go. Obviously there can be no questioning of the immense and irreversible achievements of modern science and no attempt to turn our back on the potential benefits of the technology to which it has given birth. It is necessary to say this in view of some of the purely negative elements in the thinking of the "Green" movements. What is at stake is the meaning of "knowing". It is a question of the way in which human beings are enabled to come to a true understanding of and a practical relation to the realities within which human life is set. Science does not give and does not pretend to give a complete answer to that question. But the scientific achievements of the past two hundred years have been so awe-inspiring that we have been tempted to believe that the methods of science are the sufficient key to knowledge in all its fullness. That belief has led us to the brink of disaster.

If we are controlled by the biblical vision, we shall recognize that knowledge in the fullest sense calls for commitments and attitudes which differ from those which have been lifted up as ideals during the period since the Enlightenment. The biblical vision places at the centre a relationship of trust in a personal reality much greater than ourselves. Without that trust, true knowledge of how things are will be hidden from us. There is therefore needed, if we are to break out of our present impasse, a shift in the balance between faith and doubt in the enterprise of understanding, a recognition of the fact that the critical faculty is not primary but secondary and can only operate on the basis of beliefs which are held in faith. Without this shift and this recognition, the critical faculty can only lead us into a nihilistic scepticism in which nothing is known because nothing is worth knowing.

To raise these questions will mean opening up with scientists, teachers and philosophers very large issues about the future of science and about the nature of education. Scientists have been becoming acutely aware of the fact that their work is not ethically neutral. They are much concerned about the ethical dilemmas posed for society by the results of their work. But what is needed is something more, a framework of thought in which ethical considerations are not merely external regulators of the results of scientific work, but science is itself part of a whole way of understanding from which ethics cannot be separated, because all knowing is an activity of persons responsible to God and to one another. Teachers and parents are troubled about the role of religious and moral instruction in the curriculum. Both are caught in a trap, between our scientific culture and the traditional values inherited from the Christendom era. Parents ask for religious instruction for their children, but it does not take the children long to discover that the parents do not believe what they want the children to learn. The arrival in many western schools of large numbers of children from Hindu, Sikh and Muslim homes complicates the problem, and teachers are asked to teach "religion" as an aspect of culture rather than as a vision of truth. Consequently the questions which religion might address to the "culture" which is being transmitted in the rest of the curriculum (not as part of "culture" but as "how things really are") are ruled out of order. The modern scientific world-view is taught as a true account of how things are, while religion is taught as an aspect of culture which is available in a variety of styles.

Conclusion

In the five sections of the preceding chapter I have tried to suggest some of the vast questions which are raised when our modern culture is confronted with the biblical vision of how things are. The answering of these questions must be the work of men and women expertly and deeply involved in the various disciplines of study and the various spheres of action concerned. This small essay is written as an invitation to the churches to engage together in such an effort over a period of years, possibly leading up to a major meeting at which the results of group work could be brought together.

I have started from the perception, which I believe to be valid and widely shared, that we are nearing the end of the period of 250 years during which our modern European culture has been confidently offering itself to the rest of the world as the torch-bearer for human progress. Following Polanyi, I have suggested that we are in a situation which has significant analogies with that which St Augustine faced. A uniquely brilliant culture was coming to the end of its life. It had lost the power to renew itself. What Augustine offered was nothing based upon the "self-evident" axioms of classical culture. It was a new model, a new framework for understanding and coping with experience, based upon the fact that God had become incarnate in the man Jesus and had thereby manifested and put into effect God's purpose for all history and for every human soul. That new framework was articulated in the twin dogmas of Incarnation and Trinity. It was offered as a gift to be received in faith and as the starting point for a new enterprise in understanding.

Our position is, I believe, analogous. It is not, of course, identical. We can learn from the past but we can never return to it. We must exclude any kind of nostalgia for Christendom or for a pre-technological innocence. But we can, I believe, follow the example of Augustine in being ready, boldly and without embarrassment, to offer to our dying culture the framework of understanding that has its base in the work of Jesus and to invite our contemporaries to join with us in a vigorous attempt to understand and deal with our experience afresh in the light and in the power of that name.

From the "other side"

A postscript, by Wesley Ariarajah

George Orwell's *Nineteen Eighty-four* was first published in 1949. It was a satire on modern politics, and it projected a nightmarish totalitarian future where war is peace, freedom slavery and ignorance strength. As yet there is no one single Big Brother watching all of us, but there are several, including Big Sisters as well, competing for the place.

The threat to human freedom and world peace is even greater today than when Orwell wrote his novel. At the heart of it is the crisis of western civilization, and that crisis has grown steadily worse during the last few decades.

The situation poses challenges which the churches in the west cannot evade. It raises questions about their witness which they must answer in terms of their faith. What are these questions? The formulation of the questions is a crucially important task. *The Other Side of 1984* is an attempt to raise the right questions and point to the possible answers from the perspective of the Christian faith. All of us, whether we live in the first, second or third world, must be grateful to Bishop Lesslie Newbigin for the work he has done. He has analyzed the situation, described the impasse we are in, and raised issues which we cannot afford to ignore as Christians and as human beings. The analysis is clear, the questions are sharp and the approach is bold and uncompromising.

It is important to recognize the standpoint from which Bishop Newbigin raises the questions for and on behalf of the churches. He is not simply asking: What can we do? He is not raising the academic question whether there are at all solutions to these problems in the biblical understanding of life and the world. He would rather try to identify the questions which are inevitably raised "when our modern culture is confronted with the biblical vision of how things are". This is legitimate. The only standpoint from which a theologian can raise questions is that of faith. The theologian does not ask questions in order to arrive at faith. He or she can only start by asking: What can I say to this from the perspective of my faith?

Bishop Newbigin limits the scope of the questions raised to the crisis faced by modern western culture which has grown out of the Enlightenment. He is aware that they must be answered by men and women involved in various disciplines of related study and the various spheres of concerned action.

Why a postscript

I would not presume to provide answers to the questions raised. I do not even intend to attempt an evaluation of the enquiry itself. My own limited task is to join the enquiry from the "other side" — not from beyond 1984 but from the perspective of those cultures which, though influenced by western values, are not rooted in them. And I undertake the task for three reasons.

First, because it will be of interest to consider how the questions raised here appear to a person who comes out of another culture but shares the same Christian faith. Second, because western culture has had so much to do with churches everywhere. Churches and Christian communities in every part of the world have been influenced by western cultural values — and to a much greater extent than by those who are not Christians. The issues affect them, and will affect them even more in the years ahead as they seriously grapple with questions of indigenization, interfaith dialogue, inculturation, even the concerns of mission and evangelism. Third, because it is my hope that through a postcript of this kind we can widen the scope of the whole enquiry by involving in it a much larger section of the Christian community. The book is written from within the British context. The issues it raises are seen as being common to churches in the west, but they are basically "ecumenical" issues, and an inner dialogue among the churches may help sharpen the questions and the enquiry as a whole for specific situations in all parts of the world.

I cannot hope to do justice to such a task within the limits of a brief essay. Partly because the enquiry itself is so critically important and raises such basic issues. Partly because the cultures of the world are so diverse that no one person can speak for them or on behalf of them.

Also because I am not an expert in any of the fields related to this enquiry. I must content myself with a tentative and general treatment of certain selected areas. And I shall depend in the main upon my experience in my own part of the world, the Indian sub-continent.

The impact of the west

It needs to be emphasized that the questions raised in this book are indeed important to people in other parts of the world. Western civilization based on science and technology has presented itself as the common civilization of the world, and it has had in recent years a dominant role at least in all the urban centres of the world. It was held up as the model, and it has influenced all the cultures of the world. The scientific world-view on which it was built has challenged, and in many cases undermined, the cultural foundations of a number of non-western societies. Most of the newly independent countries of the world have followed the western model of development. In fact modernization and westernization have come to mean much the same thing.

To take just one example, it was Mahatma Gandhi's great hope that India, once it achieved independence, would be built up on a village base. For him the Indian village symbolized the values and thought-frame of Indian culture. He believed that there were resources within the Indian religious tradition itself which could liberate the people and help eradicate evils like the caste system. But the government under Pandit Nehru opted for the western model. Nehru was Gandhi's disciple, but there was a vast difference between their world-views. Himself a product of the western scientific world-view, Nehru was convinced that industrialization and the scientific outlook would transform the nation, economically as well as socially and culturally. Most third world leaders have followed Nehru's example rather than Gandhi's.

Central to Bishop Newbigin's argument is the distinction between the modern scientific world-view and the world-view based on faith and authority. The distinction holds for other cultures as well. For example the rationalistic world-view is not new to India; within the six classical systems of

Indian philosophy the approach based on reason is seriously considered. However it never became the framework for Indian society. The tradition which laid down the rules of life and conduct in society *(smriti)* was expected to be drawn out of *sruti* or the truth revealed in the Vedas and the Upanishads.

Bishop Newbigin's criticism of the scientific world-view will win ready sympathy in India and other Asian countries. The roles of faith and doubt, both in understanding reality and acquiring knowledge, have been extremely complex in the Indian religious tradition, but what found overall acceptance has been the reality which stands beyond and informs reason. The ultimate meaning cannot be exhausted by what reason alone can explore. The goal of life and the meaning of happiness are similarly defined within a framework that goes beyond scientific enquiry.

In the same way, economics is primarily understood within social and ethical categories of thought. There are ethical norms related to the acquisition and utilization of wealth, and to the way in which human beings relate to nature and natural resources. The divorce between economics and ethics in the modern scientific world-view is at variance with the eastern attitude, though it must be admitted that such separation is becoming more and more evident today, thanks largely to the impact of the western civilization

A response from the other side

Bishop Newbigin identifies three fundamental features of the pre-Enlightenment period which have been undermined by the new scientific world-view. At the risk of over-simplifying the issues involved, let me summarize what he calls for.

1. We should recover the role of faith in knowing and understanding. During the Enlightenment "dogma" became a bad word; it stood for all that shackled the free exercise of human reason. The roles of faith and doubt underwent a reversal. We must recover the attitude of listening and receiving — an action of faith — as a prerequisite of knowing.

2. There is a need to recover an understanding of Christian dogma as that which can provide a framework for coming to grips with the totality of life, public as well as private. Such a faith framework should be acknowledged as having as much to do with economics and the ordering of social life as with prayer and sacraments. "Life is to be understood in its totality, that is to say as a life in which there is no dichotomy between private and public, between believer and citizen."

3. We should go back to the Bible. It is the scriptural testimony that provides perspectives for the private and public life of the Christian. It is the basis for specifically Christian judgments and actions in the public sphere.

How do these suggestions come across to one who stands, as far as it is possible to stand, outside the western civilization?

In most countries of Asia, Africa and the Middle East, the religious traditions of Hinduism, Buddhism and Islam, or a primal world-view, provide the basis for social organization. In many of these societies faith perspectives do in fact provide the overall basis for society. But there is so much distortion, injustice and misery, and people look upon science and technology as the force which can combat superstition, ignorance and conditions of servitude.

Bishop Newbigin acknowledges the positive achievements of the Enlightenment. The scientific method did indeed deliver men and women from the bondage of dogma and liberate people from a situation of virtual slavery. But today it would appear that the principles which have sustained it have run out of steam.

The question is how much of all this is applicable to non-western cultures. There are many in these cultures who see the secular scientific approach as essential for humanization and the development of people. The reasons they give need to be taken seriously.

1. A number of countries rooted in cultures other than western and drawing their social framework from faith perspectives are still, perhaps in a different sense, in the "middle ages". They still await liberation from many social and economic evils that seem part of the "fiduciary

framework" derived from their respective dogmas. There are, of course, high and lofty principles and teachings within these religious traditions, be it Hinduism, Buddism, Islam or any other traditional religion. Attempts have been made to prove that they can yield the fiduciary framework for a more just and participatory society. But despite such attempts by many reformers, these religions and cultural traditions have not been able to draw from within themselves the vitality to restructure themselves. In case after case it was the impact of modern science and a different world-view that made the difference. Somehow death seems to be an essential prerequisite for new life.

2. When one analyzes the structure of the societies that depend on dogma for their fiduciary framework, it becomes evident that dogma is interpreted and applied, not least by the priests and prophets of a given religious tradition, to enslave large sections of the people. This was true of Christianity in the middle ages, and it is still the case in many societies today. There is little room for confidence that it will not happen again, perhaps in more subtle and sophisticated ways, when the dominant role of dogma is restored. We cannot evade the issue of power; those who interpret dogma and apply it to the ordering of social life will be subject to the insidious temptation to control and dominate people.

3. The whole faith approach becomes difficult in a multi-faith, multi-cultural context where each of the religious traditions has a different fiduciary framework to offer. Interfaith dialogue and interfaith cooperation are relatively recent emphases. It is no secret that in a number of cases the impact of science and technology and its unifying, secularizing and humanizing effects have helped cultures and faiths to live together. When the fiduciary framework of one culture is different from that of another, there are only two alternatives — conversion or conflict! The long history of Protestant-Roman Catholic confrontation and Christian-Muslim conflicts must warn us against fiduciary frameworks which depend on dogmas.

The dilemma

But what does all this amount to? I do not think that these considerations in any way undermine the basic thesis that Bishop Newbigin presents. That the modern scientific world-view fails to satisfy the ultimate quest of the human being cannot be disputed. When he calls for the recovery of a faith framework to understand life and its meaning, Bishop Newbigin makes very clear that there is no question of returning to the middle ages. Indeed he argues strongly for a dialogue between modern culture and the Christian faith.

Given the ambiguity of the modern scientific method and the culture that results from it, the other cultures can learn lessons from what is happening in the west. In fact one should raise the question whether the modern scientific world-view and a fiduciary framework based on faith should be seen as alternate frameworks to choose from. The tendency to treat them as either/or seems to be at the core of the crisis facing the west. It would seem that what is important is an engagement between the modern scientific method and its application and the faith and ethical perspectives of a given society.

At first sight this would appear impossible, for they are understood as mutually exclusive. At the heart of the scientific method is the rejection of faith as a framework to understand life; it seems to rule out the possibility of dialogue between it and the faith which it seeks to exclude.

This would place the churches and peoples in other cultures in an impossible dilemma. For we cannot reject or deny the humanizing effects of science and technology; at the same time we cannot ignore the spiritual poverty and meaninglessness it seems to have produced in the western world. There is no possibility to go back to the pre-Enlightenment period, nor indeed to halt the work of human reason which goes on probing, and applying scientific methods in ways that continue to radically change life. We cannot resolve such a dilemma. The question is, can we go beyond it?

We need to put the question in this form because, at least to some observers, western culture, despite the deepening crisis, appears as standing at the brink of a new discovery. Having run its course along the principles of the scientific method, it now seems to be in a mood to look for dimensions that will give meaning to life. We should not ignore the fact that today it is not only believing Christians who are concerned over questions of seeking meaning; many scientists are groping to find meaning and purpose. Economists are beginning to be exercised over the question of human values and technologists are in a mood to seek ethical foundations for their work.

The real problem lies in the fact that we cannot go back on the scientific method and do without some of its major presuppositions. Even as there is no going back to dogma that belongs to the middle ages, there can be no return to a pre-Enlightenment scientific milieu. The recovery of faith that can meaningfully speak to modern society has to be one that integrates in it the real achievements of the new age. It should be in the idiom of a culture which, for good or ill, will continue to bear the marks that the scientific method has left on it.

Towards a dialogue with modern culture

That is why it is important to underline Bishop Newbigin's call for a dialogue with modern culture. It should be noted that in a dialogue no person has the right to assume that all the truth is only on his or her side. This should be a warning to Christians taking part in the dialogue who sometimes tend to believe that, even though dialogue involves the taking of risks, the truth revealed to them is so secure that there is no real danger of its being challenged. I wish to emphasize this point because of two reasons.

First to re-emphasize the fact that there can be no return to dogma as if nothing had happened. Dogma has indeed been badly mauled. We must recognize the role of reason to question dogma, without making reason the absolute arbiter. The relationship is dialectical.

Also, it is important to go beyond the stage of presenting reason and faith as alternatives or as mutually exclusive authorities. In some of the Indian religious traditions there is an insistence on a cluster of authorities that mutually enlighten and correct each other. Faith and reason, tradition and experience can in fact be held together as a cluster of authorities that shed light from various angles, enabling the mystery of life to be understood from many perspectives. This should be of particular interest to those of other cultures who are being challenged by the modern scientific method.

Bishop Newbigin's warning that in the process of recovering a faith framework we should not fall into the "Constantinian trap" needs to be taken with the utmost seriousness. The struggles and conflicts currently going on in the Islamic societies have their lessons for us in this context. The impact of science and technology in a number of Islamic countries has had a liberating effect on the traditional feudal society. At the same time it has also had the effect of destabilizing the fiduciary framework on which the whole society was organized. It is instructive to watch how different Islamic nations are coping with the situation. The responses range from outright rejection to accommodation and adaptation.

The problem facing Christians who live in non-western cultures is not that the societies to which they belong do not have a fiduciary framework based on faith perspectives. The problem is that they do have one, but drawn from religious persuasions other than Christian. It is of interest to note that in such situations it is the Chistians who generally favour a "secular state" in which no religion receives preferential treatment, and each is free to live and witness within its own faith framework.

Bishop Newbigin is not asking for a state run by the Church or for the Christian faith to be recognized as state religion. What he wants is a society whose economic, social, political and educational organization is based on the values and perspectives drawn from the biblical faith.

But the question for the churches in other cultures is not whether we should have a political system and social organization based on the scientific world-view or on a faith perspective. The question is "which faith framework?"

Towards a dialogue between faiths

We have the same difficulty with Bishop Newbigin's plea for the recovery of the Bible. He wants the Bible to be acknowledged as the source of the principles on which we base our social organization and specific Christian political involvement. He sees in the Bible the principles that should govern the life of individuals and societies, the promise of salvation and the basis of an ultimate hope.

While as a Christian one has full sympathy for what the Bishop stands and calls for, it is important to look at it also from the perspective of churches in cultures dominated by other living faiths.

In Sri Lanka, for example, there is constant pressure, precisely for the kind of reasons that Bishop Newbigin gives for the recovery of the biblical faith, to return to the *Buddha dhamma* as the basis of society. In many Muslim countries there are relentless attempts to reorganize society on the basis of the Quran. There is increasing pressure to make Hinduism the official religion of India so that it can become the basis of society in a more acknowledged way.

The churches in these countries face a painful dilemma. Their temptation is to opt for a secular state based on the principles of scientific knowledge so that the citizens can function with a common fiduciary framework as a nation, and at the same time have fiduciary frameworks, drawn from their respective faiths, for their private life and for the ways in which they relate to society in general. Even if one were to argue that the faith perspectives that should inform society are not derived from actual faith structures, but only from norms and values, the question remains as to whether these should be drawn from the Bible alone or from other sources as well.

It is important to enable Christians in the churches in cultures dominated by other faiths to face this question squarely and with greater honesty. It should be noted that even in dealing with the western churches Bishop Newbigin qualifies his call for a return to the Bible with the call to be in dialogue with people of other faith perceptions in their midst. The questions raised in Britain on the problem of education in multifaith communities are sufficient proof of the enormity of the problem. For the churches in other cultures it will be a much bigger and far more complex problem.

What then must we do? In a Muslim, Buddhist or a Hindu nation there can be no question of replacing their scriptures with the Bible. At the same time one sees the need for a faith perspective and recognizes the limitations of a rational scientific framework. There are some who advocate that we identify the biblical perspectives within these faiths and name them. This is a strange solution. I have never been able to understand why a Hindu perception should suddenly become "Christian" simply because a Christian is able to respond to it and accept it as biblically valid. Not only people, even principles can become victims of the proselytizing zeal!

There are others who claim that all this indicates the urgency for mission so that the other faiths, if they cannot be converted, could at least be "won over" to accept the principles on which society should be based. Quite apart from the fact that this does not give any answer to the practical problems faced by the churches today, it borders on an understanding of other faiths that leaves God altogether out of these ancient faiths. It also denies, quite unjustly, the fact that some lofty principles of organizing life and society were already present within some of the living faiths long before the advent of Christianity.

Still others would say that the churches must withdraw from the mainstream of life and become "prophetic minorities". But only participants can be prophets, and withdrawal can be a form of betrayal.

Let me outline some of the directions along which the discussion may usefully be pursued:

— The churches living in other religious cultures must theologically evaluate the faiths of others, their fiduciary frameworks, and the life-affirming values in them. They cannot hold up the biblical faith as an alternative framework to organize social life.

— The churches in other cultures need to rethink the place and role of the Bible in the context of other sacred scriptures — which are seen by others as providing equally valid guidance to organize life. They should discover

ways in which their biblical faith — the faith commitment to Jesus Christ who ministered within the faith framework of the biblical world — can be held, translated and incorporated in multifaith situations.
— The churches should ask serious questions about their relationship with other faiths. If it is obvious that in the foreseeable future, the only kind of meaningful national life is one which is inextricably bound up with the life of people of other faiths, and if it is also obvious that any fiduciary framework based on faith for the whole of life must be a common framework which can serve many religious communities, what does it mean for the churches' relationship with people of other faiths?

It is clear that all these questions point to the need for a much fuller, more genuine and more committed dialogue between faiths. In this context questions like whether dialogue is for mission, and discussions on "dialogue *or* mission", are out of place. In these situations dialogue is a fundamental service that we render to the community. Here, dialogue *is* mission; it is the only way in which Christians can participate and contribute to national life.

I have all along been conscious of the danger of distorting or misrepresenting Bishop Newbigin's thesis. Many of the questions I have raised have in fact been raised in one way or another by Bishop Newbigin himself. I have only raised them more sharply or tried to deal with them from a nonwestern perspective.

There is also the danger that a postscript like this can blunt the cutting edge of the questions raised in the original essay. Those questions remain valid to those who approach them from within the culture to which they are addressed. But because no culture today remains unaffected by other cultures, the questions become even more valid when they are raised in a broader context. All of us must face the questions that lie on the other side of 1984 and we face them more squarely if we face them together. In that process churches everywhere may also become more aware of the difficulties facing each one of them, and of the need to uphold and strengthen one another.

Printed in Switzerland